Deseret Book Company Salt Lake City, Utah

Ye Are My Friends

MARVIN J. ASHTON

ISBN 0-87747-934-8

Printed in the United States of America

10   9   8   7   6   5   4   3

To my best friend,
Norma

Contents

Contents

Foreword

When Marvin J. Ashton was ordained an apostle in December 1971, I knew that it was right. He has brought to his work a quiet dignity and the clear light of reason that enhances those around him as well as the work of the Church.

The man himself is characterized in the words he speaks and writes. This volume is characteristic of Marvin J. Ashton, a man who feels deeply about the emotional, practical, and spiritual aspects of friendship. To those who come for advice, he listens and counsels with a practical good judgment that blesses lives. In his many years of Church experience he has touched personally the lives of thousands.

In the pages of this book you will find the same wise and practical judgment that has blessed many, and through reading and heeding his counsel, you, too, can experience the same results.

I recommend to you these words of Elder Marvin J. Ashton, who is my friend.

N. ELDON TANNER

Ye Are
My Friends

Gifts of
a friend—
everlasting gifts
that will bring
joy and happiness
to those who accept them
and follow
their precepts

G

od so loved the world, that he gave his only begotten Son." (John 3:16.) And Jesus declared that he gave his life and laid it down by his own choice as an eternal gift to each one of us.

This eternal gift of the Savior was given to us as his friends. Throughout the scriptures he speaks of various individuals as "my friend." Thus we find phrases such as these: "The Lord spake unto Moses . . . as a man speaketh unto his friend" (Exodus 33:11); "the seed of Abraham my friend" (Isaiah 41:8); "Jesus said unto him, Friend" (Matthew 26:50); "I will call you friends, for ye are my friends" (D&C 93:45).

Inasmuch as we are all missionaries, before we make conversions we make friends. The Savior declared, "And again I say unto you, my friends, for from henceforth I shall call you friends, it is expedient that I give unto you this commandment, that ye become even as my friends in the days when I was with them, traveling to preach the gospel in my power." (D&C 84:77.)

Through the Prophet Joseph Smith, the Lord told the Twelve Apostles of the Church in 1832, "Ye are they whom my Father hath given me; ye are my friends." (D&C 84:63.)

As an apostle in this day, and as a friend, I would like to give you, the reader, a gift—in fact, a number of gifts; gifts that are everlasting; gifts that will, if you will accept them, bring you joy and happiness.

Gift Number One. Be united as one. Wives, husbands, children, mothers, and fathers, work together in oneness. Cleave unto each other. Care for each other. Build each other, encourage each other, be proud of each other. The Savior declared, "I say unto you, be one; and if ye are not one ye are not mine." (D&C 38:27.) The greatest place to practice oneness is in the home. "Therefore shall a man leave his father and his mother, and shall cleave unto his wife: and they shall be one flesh." (Genesis 2:24.)

Gift Number Two. Be available for consultation and communication with your family, friends, and God. Can your children talk to you? Can you talk to your parents? Can you talk to your God? Be available to communicate and have relationships verbally and of the spirit with those about you. May I share this powerful scripture from Hebrews 13:16 to clinch my point: "To do good and to communicate forget not: for with such sacrifices God is well pleased." Take time to make yourself available for the purposes of the Lord.

Gift Number Three. Be free of criticism and murmuring. Build and lift in your words and conversations as you sustain and support. Murmuring and criticism lead to inactivity and apostasy from the Church. Do not allow yourself the dangerous luxury of criticism and murmuring. When I think of those who are prone to murmur, I think of Laman and Lemuel. "And thus Laman and Lemuel, being the eldest, did murmur against their father. And they did murmur because they knew not the dealings of

that God who had created them." (1 Nephi 2:12.)
Often murmuring is an outward evidence of dis-
obedience.

Gift Number Four. Be a full tithe payer and honest with God and men in all of your money matters.
Some people say they pay tithing because they want
to receive blessings. I want you to know that I pay my
tithing because I want to be obedient. If we are obedient, we do not have to worry about blessings. If we
are obedient, the blessings will come naturally and
irrevocably. "Will a man rob God? Yet ye have
robbed me. But ye say, Wherein have we robbed
thee? In tithes and offerings." (Malachi 3:8.) "Those
who have thus been tithed shall pay one-tenth of all
their interest annually; and this shall be a standing
law unto them forever, for my holy priesthood, saith
the Lord." (D&C 119:4.)

Gift Number Five. Be conscientious in your reading and study of the scriptures and all good books.
Make study a daily habit. Make good books your
friends. Avoid trash literature at all times. Those
who participate in pornographic reading and pic-
tures will be stricken by the disease caused by that
kind of behavior. What does the Lord say about
good books and reading? Let me share a quotation
from the Doctrine and Covenants: "And as all have
not faith, seek ye diligently and teach one another
words of wisdom; yea, seek ye out of the best books
words of wisdom; seek learning, even by study and
also by faith." (D&C 88:118.)

Gift Number Six. Be a Sabbath day observer.
Keep the Sabbath day holy. Often the best rest you
can have is on a day when you think of no one but
others. "And the inhabitants of Zion shall also ob-

serve the Sabbath day to keep it holy." (D&C 68:29.) Through this gift of Sabbath observance, I promise you blessings mentally, spiritually, and physically.

Gift Number Seven. Be a leader who stays within the channels of priesthood authority. There is safety and wisdom in proper procedure. One of the strongest channels of help in the Church is found within the channels of strength in the home.

Gift Number Eight. Be an individual who can keep a trust. Be able to maintain a confidence. Remember, it is greater to be trusted than loved. A trust is sacred. "It is better to trust in the Lord than to put confidence in man." (Psalm 118:8.)

Gift Number Nine. Bear your testimony regularly to the divinity of Jesus Christ and His church. Your testimony, properly shared, will lift, lead, and reassure. The more you honestly share your testimony with others, the more you will have left. Testimonies can grow only as they are shared. "Behold, verily I say unto you, for this cause I have sent you—that you might be obedient, and that your hearts might be prepared to bear testimony of things which are to come." (D&C 58:6.)

Gift Number Ten. Be a leader in integrity, dignity, poise, punctuality, and love for the right. The Lord loves those who lead by example. Let your personal conduct be first class. Let your conduct be worthy of a Latter-day Saint. Allow yourself to so live that you are good for yourself. One of the favorites of our Savior, Jesus Christ, during the restoration period in the early days of the Church was Hyrum Smith. Do you know why the Savior, Jesus Christ, loved Hyrum Smith? Let me tell you why. "Blessed is my servant Hyrum Smith; for I, the

Lord, love him because of the integrity of his heart, and because he loveth that which is right before me." (D&C 124:15.)

Gift Number Eleven. Be a listener, even one who has ears to hear and to learn. Take the time to listen to family members, to friends, to the stranger, to the weary, and to God. Some people become so wise, so they think, that they go forward without believing they have to listen to God. God listens. Were he not willing to listen, he would not invite us to pray. Make listening a more important part of your prayers. "But to be learned is good, if they hearken unto the counsels of God." (2 Nephi 9:29.)

Gift Number Twelve. Be courageous enough to be a real Latter-day Saint in living and defending the truth that you know. When you are keeping commandments and walking in his paths, you have no need to fear. Have the courage to stand by the right. As you stand by the right, you will never have to stand alone.

I humbly pray that you will be willing and ready and able to accept these gifts—gifts everlasting—gifts that will bring you joy and happiness.

We Serve
That Which
We Love

What we learn
to love
can make or break
our lives

Just before six o'clock one morning, my wife and I boarded a taxi in San Francisco during a short layover on a trip to Salt Lake City from Australia. Our driver, who had been on duty since three o'clock that morning, was anxious to talk with us, his first passengers of the day. We learned that his parents, who were born just outside Mexico City, moved to Chicago, where he was born, and then to New Mexico. Twenty years earlier our friend had come for a short visit to San Francisco and had never left. During our trip to the airport, he related a few incidents from which some great truths were reemphasized.

His parents, he told us, had remained in New Mexico, but they liked to visit him and his brother whenever they could afford it because they loved being with their children and grandchildren. In New Mexico his mother's health was rather poor, but whenever she was in San Francisco, she seemed to feel much better. This discerning son had said to his brother, "I know exactly what mother needs." Then he told us, "I found a large truck, and my brother and I drove to New Mexico. We loaded our parents and all their possessions into the truck, and brought them to live near those who loved them most. Mother's health improved noticeably." Then he added, "You know, love is very important if it is done right."

The second incident related by this humble but wise man is also significant. He said, "I teach all my children to work. I want them to have schooling, but they must learn to work to get it. I just finished helping my sixteen-year-old son get a part-time job at a bank. While he is going to school, he only works two hours a day, but he is learning to work. He knows I love him, because I do my part too. Because of the uncertainty of my driving hours, I can't always take him to work, but I'm always there to bring him home. He looks forward to our ride together, and so do I."

One other important point was made by this unusual taxi operator. He told us that some of his unmarried friends who are also taxi drivers are often out of money. They come to him to borrow, and he indicated that he is generally able to help them. When his companions ask how he is able to support his family on his salary when they can't even keep themselves, he said, "I don't waste money at the races or on liquor or tobacco. My wife fixes our meals at home, so we don't have to pay for expensive restaurant food." He smiled when he added, "We do our partying with our family." This man's objectives are family oriented, and he has learned the folly of serving momentary expensive habits.

A happy man, this driver. He has realized through experience important areas of love. He knows that nurturing love is healing; it is teaching. He knows that such love requires sacrifice, and that which we love will be that to which we give our allegiance. He shared with us some basic principles of love in action that were potent. Frankly, we were enjoying his comments so much that we almost wished the airport terminal were another half hour away.

This taxi driver knew where to place his love. We, too, must choose carefully the areas in which we serve, because where we serve, there will be our love. During our lifetime, areas of love must be put in proper perspective.

In childhood we anxiously strive to ride that bicycle, to skate, to ski, to learn the laws of balance. Then our love of wheels and speed and balance becomes one of the joys of life. As we mature and serve and sacrifice for other interests, new loves develop. A farmer grows to love his land; a scholar, his books; a businessman, his company. We have all witnessed the love of parents for their children, the love of a bishop for members of his ward, the love of a young man for his new car, the love of a newly engaged woman for the ring received from someone very special.

Equally apparent in the world today is love many have for that which is evil. We jeopardize our future by loving and sacrificing for that which is not conducive to our health or our progress.

Many today are caught up in their love for worldly goods that they think will bring them fame, fortune, and popularity. They, too, reap the rewards of loving incorrectly, for that which they serve they will learn to love. What we learn to love can make or break our lives.

Love of money, drugs, and alcohol can turn men into thieves, murderers, and derelicts. First they love the effects of those evil things, then they sacrifice all—life, health, and liberty—for that which they think are treasures. Love of the sensual, of drugs, and of lies grows as we serve in these areas made so appealing by Satan. Bonds of love become strong and intense in proportion to our continuing service. A man who learns to love a lie serves dishonesty all his life. In fact, a drug addict can usually be cured more quickly than can a liar.

One of the greatest accomplishments of Satan in these last days is his success in turning men's affection toward the destructive, the fleeting, the worldly. Rather than planning for that which is best for all, the world is becoming increasingly "me" centered. On every hand we hear many group leaders say, "We have a right," "We demand." Many young people believe that love has "rights" one can demand of a loved one. For example, a young man may say, "If you love me, you will let me . . ." He would take what he supposes are his rights rather than serving the higher standards of morality. Such a request does not bespeak love. Day-to-day acts of service, whether for good or evil, may not seem important, but they build cords of love that become so strong they can seldom be broken. Our responsibility is to place our areas of love in proper perspective. Meaningful love always works for our eternal progress and not against it.

One who loves has and feels responsibility. The apostle Paul says that love "suffereth long, and is kind; . . . seeketh not her own, . . . thinketh no evil." (1 Corinthians 13:4-5.) If we look at love between two people who are preparing for temple marriage, we see the elements of sacrifice and of serving each other's best interest, not a short-sighted "me" interest. True love and happiness in courtship and marriage are based upon honesty, self-respect, sacrifice, consideration, courtesy, kindness, and placing "we" ahead of "me." Those who would have us forfeit virtue and chastity to prove our love in participating in sex out of wedlock are neither friends nor eternal-family oriented. To classify them as selfish and unwise is not too severe. Those who serve the flesh will never know the love and fruits of purity.

A new convert to the Church recently shared this story: "I was in and out of enforced confinement most of my teen years. It wasn't so bad being there, because the food was pretty good, and we were treated all right. But it did get boring, so when anyone had any reading material, funny books, magazines, or anything, we would trade our food for a chance to borrow those items. One day I saw a fellow with a nice, thick book. I knew it would take a long time to read, so I offered him my pork chops, my potatoes, and all my main course food items for a week. He accepted my offer and loaned me the book. As I read it, I knew I was reading something very special and very true. The book for which I had sacrificed my food was titled the Book of Mormon. When I had a chance, I found the missionaries, changed my habits, and am now finding a new way of life. I love that book for which I traded my food."

Here was an unusual but worthwhile sacrifice with rewarding results. This convert indicated that the more time he spends with this book, the greater his love becomes for the truths he is finding between its covers.

Choose ye carefully what and whom you will serve or for what you will sacrifice, because that is where your love will be placed. It is important not only to love well, but also to love prudently. What we love takes our time. That to which we give time, we are apt to love. Our daily actions determine where our love will be.

Love for one's family is not the love of a martyr. Think back about the practical sermon of our taxi driver: "I teach my children to work, but I let them know I care. I do my part too." Our time, the listening ear, the understanding heart, and the unconditional love, even the opening of doors of opportunity at times, are some ways to serve those we love. But if we deprive family members of opportunity for their own actions, if we use them to further our own ambitions, then we do not serve them well or love them prudently. Wise love of family and people takes time.

If you give a child an opportunity to work and contribute in the home, his love of family will increase. As he is encouraged to give time and sacrifice to develop his talents, whether they be academic or in music, drama, sports, leadership, or whatever, he will develop a love for that which brings him success. Children will love those talents or possessions to which we encourage them to give time and effort.

As adults, if our top priorities are constantly directed toward the acquisition of more and better worldly goods, it will not take long to increase our love in those directions. The purchase of a larger house or a nicer car or a more expensive boat may cause us to sacrifice our resources and develop an unwise love for these symbols of success and pleasure. We learn to love that which we serve, and we serve that which we love.

How can we decrease our love for things not for our best good? We must examine our lives and see what services we are rendering and what sacrifices we are making, and then stop the expenditure of time and effort in these directions. If this can be managed, that love will wither and die. Our love should be channeled into sources that are eternally oriented. Our neighbors and families will respond to our love if we will but follow through with sustaining support and self-sharing. True love is as eternal as life itself. Some callings and assignments in the Church may seem insignificant and unimportant at the time, but with each willingly fulfilled assignment, love of the Lord will grow. We learn to love God as we serve and know Him.

How can we help a new convert to learn to love the gospel? By finding ways for him to serve and sacrifice. We must constantly emphasize the truth that we love that to which we give time, whether it be the gospel, God, or gold. Often we hear expressions of love for the scriptures, including Jesus' teachings. Those who study, practice, and apply the truths not only know them best, but are also fortified to use them for guidance all along life's paths. The man who most appreciates the opportunity to pay tithing is he who experiences the joys and blessings that come through sacrifice, application, and obedience to the law of the tithe. Our appreciation and love of the gospel and its teachings will always be in proportion to our service and commitment to the gospel.

The greatest example of love available to all of us is, of course, found in the scriptures: "For God so loved the world that he gave his only begotten Son." (John 3:16.) By the greatest of all acts of love and by this supreme sacrifice, God set the pattern. He demonstrated to us that His love is unconditional and is sufficient to encircle every person.

While Jesus was on earth, He taught us ways to use love correctly. We recall that when the scribes and Pharisees brought before Him a woman taken in adultery, their purpose was not to show love for either the woman or Jesus, but to embarrass and trick Him. They quoted the law of Moses, which said, "Such should be stoned," and asked of the Master, "What sayest thou?" The accusers walked away one by one when Jesus encouraged the one without sin to cast the first stone. We recall that Jesus asked of the woman, "Where are those thine accusers? hath no man condemned thee?" She answered, "No man, Lord." And Jesus said to her, "Neither do I condemn thee: go, and sin no more." (John 8:3-11.)

Jesus did not condone adultery—there is no doubt about His attitude toward moral conduct. He chose to teach with love, to show the scribes and Pharisees the need of serving the individual for her best good, and to show how destructive are trickery and embarrassment. He demonstrated to us that under all circumstances there is a proper way to show love. Perhaps our taxi driver has learned to apply the same Christian principle in his life when he wisely said, "You know, love is very important if it is done right." The Savior's conduct would entitle all of us to conclude that love is right when it is channeled to proper areas and given the right priority in our lives.

We live in a complex world where many forces are calling out, "Love me." A sure way to set our guidelines for that which we choose to serve and learn to love is to follow the admonition of Joshua: "As for me and my house, we will serve the Lord." (Joshua 24:15.) Let us look to our own lives. We serve that which we love. If we sacrifice and give our love for that which our Father in heaven asks of us, our footsteps will be set upon the path of eternal life. May God help us to love the right, love the truth, and love areas of service that are rewarding and eternal.

Yellow Ribbons and Charted Courses

Our Heavenly Father wants us to move forward without the spirit of fear

Some years ago an interesting account appeared in a New Zealand newspaper about a family of four and their ocean voyage. In a well-stocked thirty-five-foot sloop they departed on an extended trip. After a few days out, their boat struck a reef off New Caledonia. The four occupants managed to get into a life raft with some water, food, and a radio before the yacht was lost. After some anxious hours, their radio distress signal was picked up in New Caledonia. Before long, they were reached by an air/sea rescue helicopter.

When the four family members were safely ashore and being interviewed by reporters, the woman kept repeating, "We've lost everything! We've lost everything! Everything we had was in that sailboat. All of our money, our clothes, and our possessions are gone. And the yacht was not insured. We've lost everything!"

Earl Nightingale, a well-known philosopher, in reporting this story commented on the lack of proper preparation of which this family was guilty. Reefs in the South Pacific are well charted. Insurance is always available, and learning the skills of sailing should be part of training processes before venturing out into open seas.

Our Heavenly Father wants us to move forward without the spirit of fear. The Apostle Paul wrote to Timothy, "For God hath not given us the spirit of fear, but of power, and of love, and of a *sound mind.*" (2 Timothy 1:7. Italics added.)

A sound mind to me means using our ability to think, to plan, to work, and to chart our course as we sail through the seas of life. If we are smart, we will prepare well for either the smooth sailing or the hidden reefs and the troubled waters.

Let me tell you about a young woman who charted her course ahead of time. A recently called member of a bishopric with his lovely wife at his side thankfully related this situation: "She deserves much of the credit for my present course in life. When we were dating years ago, I took her for a ride in my car to a secluded area. We parked. As I started to make some intimate advances that she felt were improper, she said, 'All my life I have planned on being married in the temple. Don't you disqualify me!'" She had charted her course before she got into troubled waters.

Certainly preparation precedes power, and if we can prepare ourselves, we have no need to fear. The present and the future belong to those who have the power that comes through preparation.

Recall with me, if you will, the power that Queen Esther used to save her people.

King Ahasuerus, who "reigned, from India even unto Ethiopia," invited all his princes as well as his servants to a feast. He asked some of his servants to bring his wife, Queen Vashti, before his guests so they could look upon her beauty. But she refused to come. The king, extremely angry, decided to put this queen away. He then called for all the fair virgins of his kingdom to be brought before him. Esther, a Jewish girl, was brought in, and she found favor with the king. The Bible says, "And the king loved Esther above all the women, and she obtained grace and favour in his sight . . . so that he set the royal crown upon her head, and made her queen instead of Vashti."

In the royal court was a high official named Haman. He became angry when Esther's uncle, Mordecai, didn't bow down to him, so he convinced the king that he (Haman) should be given authority to destroy all the Jews throughout the kingdom.

Mordecai, who had raised Esther, got word to the queen about the order to exterminate her people. He asked her to go to the king to make supplication for the Jews. The King did not know that Esther was a Jewess.

Esther was very frightened, for the penalty for going to the king without an invitation was death unless the king held out his golden scepter. However, Mordecai told her that her people were in great danger of being destroyed if she did not go, "and who knoweth whether thou art come to the kingdom for such a time as this?"

To help prepare herself for the task, Esther asked all the Jews and her handmaidens to fast with her for three days. Then she said, "And so will I go in unto the king, which is not according to the law: and if I perish, I perish."

On the third day Esther put on her royal apparel and went before the king. He held out his golden scepter and asked, "What wilt thou, queen Esther?" He told her she could have anything she wished: "It shall be even given thee to the half of the kingdom." Esther replied that she would like to invite both the king and Haman to a banquet that she had prepared. At the banquet Esther told the king of Haman's evil plans to destroy her people. The king, who loved Esther very much, gave orders that the Jews could defend themselves, and Haman and his forces then backed down. And "the Jews had light, and gladness, and joy, and honour" in the kingdom. (See Esther 1–9.)

Queen Esther knew deep fear at that time in her life, yet she was able to achieve her goal. She used her power to save her people. She turned to God for help. She asked her people to use their faith and power in her behalf. By so doing, she found the strength to move forward without fear and to use her power righteously. Our Heavenly Father has given that same power to all members of the Church. Each of us has the capacity to influence those around us for good or for evil. The key to that power is found in love.

Today there is a sister in Australia whose name is not Esther, but she too influenced a man to become great. After an extended courtship, the young man thought the time was right to propose marriage. In response to his proposal, the young woman said, "If you marry me, it will have to be in the temple." He, a nonmember, said, "What is a temple?" He found out. Months later they were married in the temple. Today this woman of influence stands at his side as the wife of one of our very successful stake presidents. Her actions, like Esther's, are helping many Latter-day Saints in the "land down under" to be saved and find their way back to their Father in heaven because she courageously used her power to influence for good.

Another member of the stake presidency said,

"My wife has had much to do with this special calling that is now mine. When we were dating and I was inactive in the Church, I gained the courage one night to ask her if she would marry me. She didn't say yes and she didn't say no. She said, 'Where?' I spent the next number of months squaring myself around so I could take her to the temple. She had made her plans, and I loved her enough to rechart my course to coincide with hers. I knew what to do and where I had to go if I wanted to travel at her side."

Some time ago yellow ribbons waved over much of the United States to welcome home with love fifty-two persons who had been held hostage for over a year in Iran. Jimmy Lopez, one of the hostages, said as he arrived home in Phoenix, Arizona, "I just can't believe this! This is what it is all about. When it gets right down to it, we stick together."

All the hostages seemed to be buoyed up by the spirit of love that our Father in heaven has given to all of us to share. To grow, this spirit must be used— not just for 444 days to fifty-two Americans in Iran, but day by day and hour by hour toward ourselves, our families, and our neighbors.

The woman whose boat was lost mourned that she had nothing left, even though her husband and children were safe and standing at her side. Do you think her sense of values and spirit of love were misplaced?

President N. Eldon Tanner, in his general conference talk in April 1967, said, "As we look back over our life, whether it be short or long, we realize that the thing that gave the greatest joy was doing something for someone else because we loved him." (*Improvement Era,* June 1967, p. 29.)

When we make our own selves better day by day, we are exhibiting the spirit of love. Jesus said, "A new commandment I give you, That ye love one another; as I have loved you, that ye also love one another." (John 13:34.) To appreciate that no one is just like us, that no one is any more important, that no one is any more needed or valuable than we are, is to magnify that spirit. Mistakes are made, and when they are corrected, we grow through the process. The true spirit of love won't let us diminish our love of self as we change and improve. Love of others can often result in our helping them choose the right and gain needed self-respect.

No one can choose or chart our course for us—that is our right, our responsibility, our opportunity. As we feel that spirit of love that God has given to us, we might examine our resources and make reachable goals. One way is to take a pencil and paper at the beginning of each week and to list realistic ways in which we can and will express love to ourselves as well as to others around us. *Love* is such a vague word. To reap the benefits of loving, specific actions must be taken. The hungry man must not be pitied—he must be fed. The lonesome young woman needs not just a quick smile—she needs someone to walk with her, arm in arm. The tired mother needs not just a valentine saying "I love you"—she needs to be given help with daily tasks. We are told to love our neighbors. There are many ways to show love: a compliment, a kind word, a loaf of bread, a visit, a listening ear. "As I have loved you . . . love one another."

Yes, love is the key to overcoming fear. In the Doctrine and Covenants we read, "Therefore, be ye strong from henceforth; fear not, for the kingdom is yours." (D&C 38:15.) This is a great promise. Fear is a stifling feeling, a roadblock. It comes not from God. Through power from God that is ours for the asking, we can overcome fear and have the courage to move forward. The spirit of love, the yellow ribbons, hugs, smiles, kindnesses, service, knowing that people are more important than possessions—these add flowers, sunshine, and joy as we travel along the road to our inheritance in the kingdom of God.

The gospel is the chart to study as we make our plans. From it can come our compass and our maps. Just as the charts were there for the family from New Zealand to study, but which they chose to ignore, so may we use the gospel of Jesus Christ to chart our life's course or ignore it. Our Father in heaven offers it, but He won't force it on us.

This is a great time to be alive. God lives. He loves us and wants us to be happy. I look forward to tomorrow, next week, next month, and next year with enthusiasm. Join me in facing all of our tomorrows with excitement and anticipation. God has not only reserved us to be upon the earth at this time, but many of His greatest wonders are yet to be performed. We can be and are entitled to be part of the action with Him. He lives, and He wants us to move forward from where we are today without fear, and in power, love, and intelligence.

It's No Fun
Being Poor

What we do
with what we have
is more important
than what
we actually have

One of life's great lessons is to teach us that what we do with what we have is more important than what we actually have. If we have the proper incentives and attitudes, we need never classify ourselves as poor. However, if we are not wise in our daily conduct, we can become victims of real poverty. It's no fun being poor!

Here are ten truths to help each of us avoid being poor, ten truths that, if applied in our lives through proper self-motivation, can help each of us overcome and avoid poverty in our lives.

1. *Thou shalt not lose a friend or cease being one.*

A person is poor when he is friendless. When friends, those closest to us, have cause to desert, to disbelieve, and to lose confidence in us, we are poor. Often friends are lost because we are unwilling to pay the price it takes to maintain them. It was Emerson who said, "The only way to have a friend is to be one." A friend is a person who will not only take the time to know us, but will also take the time to be with us, and who never leaves us regardless of the circumstances.

One of the finest presents each us of can give someone else is our best self. When we lose a friend, our strength as well as our desire is often totally drained. In our personal balance sheets, "minus friends" indicates a loss position. No man is useless while he has a friend. No man can declare personal bankruptcy if he has one friend.

A friend is a priceless possession because a true friend is one who is willing to take us the way we are but is able to leave us better than he found us. We are poor when we lose friends, because generally they are willing to reprove, admonish, love, encourage, and guide for our best good. A friend lifts the heavy heart, says the encouraging word, and assists in supplying our daily needs. As friends, we make ourselves available without delay to those who need us.

It is hoped that in the days ahead more and more of us will free ourselves from such expressions as "If you need me, let me know," or "If I can be of help, call me," and replace them with the development of a sixth sense that will let us know when and where our friendship is needed.

When Joseph Smith was in the Liberty Jail, he poured out his heart and soul, crying, "O God, where art thou?" Part of God's great declaration of love and encouragement to him at that time was: "My son, . . . thy friends do stand by thee, and they shall hail thee again with warm hearts and friendly hands. Thou art not yet as Job; thy friends do not contend against thee, neither charge thee with transgression, as they did Job." (D&C 121:7, 9-10.) The Prophet was enduring much for God's own purposes, but he was rich because his friends were standing by him.

A person is poor when he is friendless, but even poorer when he ceases to be a friend. No matter what the conduct or negligence of others may be, we cannot afford to yield in our sincere pursuit to be a

friend. Often our family members and friends need
our friendship most when they deserve it least.

2. *Thou shalt honor thy character and protect it from
self-destruction.*

A person is poor if his character is honey-
combed with greed and warped by dishonesty.
When one yields to misconduct under pressure, he
is poor. An individual who sells his character and
reputation for cash, honor, or convenience is
headed for personal bankruptcy. When one thinks
getting by is a substitute for doing his best, he is poor
in character.

A person who has to beg for bread is not poor if
he has not bent to expediency. Virtue, action, and
truth, properly blended in life, make one rich. Our
character is determined by how we perform in meeting life's challenges. Thank God for those who have
the courage to stand up and be counted on the side
of truth and integrity. What a compliment it is to
have someone say to us, "He will not yield his principles under pressure or distress."

3. *Thou shalt not deceive.*

Sir Walter Scott said, "Oh, what a tangled web
we weave/When first we practice to deceive!"
(*Lochinvar*, st. 7.) A man of character considers what
is right. A man of deceit asks, "What will partial
truths bring me when I crowd the line of truth?"

In a revelation through the Prophet Joseph
Smith, the Lord declared: "And again, verily I say
unto you, blessed is my servant Hyrum Smith; for I,
the Lord, love him because of the integrity of his
heart, and because he loveth that which is right before me." (D&C 124:15.)

A favorite tool of the devil is deception. He

would have us all become poor by living and promoting the lie. Whenever deception is encouraged,
the promoter is the greatest loser. He must bear the
responsibility for those he injures. Satan's skills win
him the title "father of deceit."

4. *Thou shalt not compromise thy principles.*

Character has been defined as education properly applied. The sharing and encouraging of truth
on a continuing basis shelters one from poverty. No-
bility in character is one asset that will bring divi-
dends regardless of the business climate. A quality
person will not compromise his principles regardless of the size or intensity of the foe or situation. In a
sense, a person who compromises advertises that a
certain price or consideration will cause him to sell
out. People of uncompromising principles are never
poor. How rich are those who can live by worthy
principles and manage the results.

5. *Thou shalt love thyself.*

A person is poor when he loses self-dignity, self-
respect, and self-pride. How sad, how long the day
when we become low on ourselves. The worst form
of defeat is to be conquered by self. Defeat is not
pleasant, but nothing is so painful and devastating as
self-defeat. A person is poor when he places despair
over hope. To lose our self-dignity and self-respect
is the worst form of poverty. When trust in friends
and trust in self are both lost, not much is left in life.
We should teach, particularly ourselves, that nobody is a nobody. We are someone, and with God's
help we can accomplish all things. How unwise, how
unfair to sell ourselves short when God is our part-
ner. Personal bankruptcy is impossible for a person
of self-pride. A person is truly rich when he remem-

bers who he really is and remembers his relationship
to God, family, and self.

6. *Thou shalt be honest.*

A person is poor when he thinks honesty is a
policy instead of a proper way of life. An honest con-
science is worth more than it costs. Greatness is measured by honest self-appraisal. "What shall it profit a
man, if he shall gain the whole world, and lose his
own soul?" (Mark 8:36.) How many times have you
heard the declaration that it is greater to be trusted
than to be loved? Let me remind you that regardless
of the number of times, you haven't heard it
enough. One of my greatest pleadings with the Lord
on a daily basis is for Him to help me turn the hearts
of the dishonest to repentance. Without honesty,
there is no foundation upon which to build. How
can a person be helped when he insists on living the
lie? Lying and living the lie keep us poor.

7. *Thou shalt not wrongfully exploit others for personal advantage.*

A person is poor when he drops or uses the
name of an individual or an institution to promote
or sell his questionable wares. How unfair, unwise,
and poor are those who would have us believe that a
get-rich investment opportunity is desirable because
of the ecclesiastical office of the one who is making
the proposition. Any person who allows his good
name or image to be used to promote or encourage
schemes of the unscrupulous is embracing dishonesty. A lie is any communication given to another
with the intent to deceive. Flattery, failure to defend
a truth or principle, failure to discipline, and the en-
dorsement of a fallacy are a few other forms of ex-
ploiting for personal gain.

In today's marketplace, scheming, deceiving promoters are making available to gullible purchasers, all kinds of enticing offers. We are sorry to report that thousands within our ranks are being duped by the glib tongues of those who offer and solicit in whispers "once in a lifetime" opportunities and "just for you" approaches. Those who give such glib promoters even the time of day are moving in the direction of being poor.

8. *Thou shalt not believe repentance is an announcement.*

A person is poor when he lives by comparison rather than by principle. A person is poor when he fails to realize that repentance is a process and not just a declaration. Every person has the challenge of recognizing and carrying his personal cross and then going forth. Repentance is an action principle, not a self-declared holding pattern.

One who is willing to repent will never have more liabilities than assets. Repentance makes it possible for the sinner to get back up when he falls. True repentance doesn't allow a person to stay poor. When important happenings and decisions in life come our way and we feel we are at the very valley in our life's travels, we always have the choice of either repenting or rebelling. A person is poor only when he is unwilling to use and understand repentance. Repentance is a major stepping stone in becoming rich. Repentance is not an announcement—it is improved conduct.

9. *Thou shalt not stay poor.*

It's not fun being poor, but no one has to be. With friends, virtue, character, truth, integrity, repentance, and other God-given gifts and rights available, pearls of great price are ours for the seeking. Through prayer and action, God helps us avoid being poor. He who has eternal life in its fulness is rich. It's no fun being poor. It is much more fun to be rich. We can be rich if life's ledger is filled with daily entries with bottom line totals that show sound moral conduct, uprightness, and incorruptibility.

10. *Thou shalt not allow thyself to be managed by money.*

Remember, those who are financially well-to-do are poor when they allow their money to manage them instead of them managing their money. No matter how much or how little we have to live on, we need to use our money wisely. We need to budget and live within it. Some claim that living within a budget takes the fun out of life and is too restrictive. Those who avoid the inconvenience of budget regulations must suffer the pains of living outside of it. Budget guidelines encourage better performance and management. There will always be emergencies and crises in life that cause financial drain, but even these developments need not make us poor. Having friends, family, neighbors, and Church associates who care and share makes us rich. Financial disaster can be avoided if we learn how to help ourselves. Personal satisfaction can be realized as we make appropriate use of the accumulation of this world's goods. No one needs to apologize for his success in financial achievement if the means of attainment have been honorable and he knows how to wisely use what he has.

Conversely, when money and wealth become our goal and our god, we are poor. I personally applaud those who are successful in achieving an abundance of this world's goods, but only if it is convincingly evident their money is being wisely used. No one should be respected just for his riches, but rather by his philanthropy. We do not judge the value of the sun by its height, but for its use.

May Heavenly Father bless us with this world's goods, but not with more than we can bear. It's no fun being poor. Fortunately, none of us has to be.

Your
Great Worth

With God's help
we can accomplish
all things,
and our potential
is unlimited

In The Church of Jesus Christ of Latter-day Saints, the individual, the human soul, is of utmost importance. We are the sons and daughters of God. He loves us. He wants us to have joy and happiness and to be exalted and dwell with Him. He has said, "This is my work and my glory—to bring to pass the immortality and eternal life of man." (Moses 1:39.) "Remember the worth of souls is great in the sight of God." (D&C 18:10.)

Each of us and our life are most important to God. We all need to be reminded of this great fact. His church, His truths, and His eternal dwelling places are for those who love Him, keep His commandments, and continue in His word. "For behold, the Lord your Redeemer suffered death in the flesh; wherefore he suffered the pain of all men, that all men might repent and come unto him. And he hath risen again from the dead, that he might bring all men unto him, on conditions of repentance." (D&C 18:11-12.)

One of the greatest daily evidences we have of God's great love for each of us is our relationship to Him in our prayers. He has invited us to pray constantly. He wants to hear from us. He wants to help us. He wants to guide us. He wants us to be dependent upon him. He wants us to pray always for guidance, strength, and constant protection. Nephi taught:

"And now, my beloved brethren, I perceive that ye ponder still in your hearts; and it grieveth me that I must speak concerning this thing. For if ye would hearken unto the Spirit which teacheth a man to pray ye would know that ye must pray; for the evil spirit teacheth not a man to pray, but teacheth him that he must not pray. But behold, I say unto you that ye must pray always, and not faint; that ye must not perform any thing unto the Lord save in the first place ye shall pray unto the Father in the name of Christ, that he will consecrate thy performance unto thee, that thy performance may be for the welfare of thy soul." (2 Nephi 32:8-9.)

We should never underestimate the power of prayer. We are members of the Church of Christ today because God heard the prayers of a fourteen-year-old boy. Joseph Smith is a prophet of God, and God heard his prayers. I thank the Lord every day of my life for the powerful scripture found in James 1:5-7, which led Joseph to kneel in prayer:

"If any of you lack wisdom, let him ask of God, that giveth to all men liberally, and upbraideth not; and it shall be given him. But let him ask in faith, nothing wavering. For he that wavereth is like a wave of the sea driven with the wind and tossed. For let not that man think that he shall receive any thing of the Lord."

Joseph later wrote:

"Never did any passage of scripture come with more power to the heart of man than this did at this time to mine. It seemed to enter with great force into every feeling of my heart. I reflected on it again and again, knowing that if any person needed wisdom from God, I did; for how to act I did not know; for the teachers of religion of the different sects understood the same passages of scripture so differently as to destroy all confidence in settling the question by an appeal to the Bible.

"At length I came to the conclusion that I must either remain in darkness and confusion, or else I must do as James directs, that is, ask of God. I at length came to the determination to 'ask of God,' concluding that if he gave wisdom to them that lacked wisdom, and would give liberally, and not upbraid, I might venture.

"So, in accordance with this, my determination to ask of God, I retired to the woods to make the attempt. It was on the morning of a beautiful, clear day, early in the spring of eighteen hundred and twenty. It was the first time in my life that I had made such an attempt, for amidst all my anxieties I had never as yet made the attempt to pray vocally.

"After I had retired to the place where I had previously designed to go, having looked around me, and finding myself alone, I kneeled down and began to offer up the desire of my heart to God. I had scarcely done so, when immediately I was seized upon by some power which entirely overcame me, and had such an astonishing influence over me as to bind my tongue so that I could not speak. Thick darkness gathered around me, and it seemed to me for a time as if I were doomed to sudden destruction.

"But, exerting all my powers to call upon God to deliver me out of the power of this enemy which had seized upon me, and at the very moment when I was ready to sink into despair and abandon myself to destruction—not to an imaginary ruin, but to the power of some actual being from the unseen world, who had such marvelous power as I had never before felt in any being—just at this moment of great alarm, I saw a pillar of light exactly over my head, above the brightness of the sun, which descended gradually until it fell upon me.

"It no sooner appeared than I found myself delivered from the enemy which held me bound. When the light rested upon me I saw two Personages, whose brightness and glory defy all description, standing above me in the air. One of them spake unto me, calling me by name and said, pointing to the other—*This is My Beloved Son. Hear Him!*

"My object in going to inquire of the Lord was to know which of all the sects was right, that I might know which to join. No sooner, therefore, did I get possession of myself, so as to be able to speak, than I asked the Personages who stood above me in the light, which of all the sects was right (for at this time it had never entered into my heart that all were wrong)—and which I should join.

"I was answered that I must join none of them, for they were all wrong; and the Personage who addressed me said that all their creeds were an abomination in his sight; that those professors were all corrupt; that: 'they draw near to me with their lips, but their hearts are far from me, they teach for doctrines the commandments of men, having a form of godliness, but they deny the power thereof.'" (Joseph Smith—History 1:12-19.)

God answers prayers today in the home, in the

office, in the school, on the highway, in the air, in our dating, in our courtships, in our churches and temples, and in our solitude and ponderings. We must pray constantly that we might know God, His plans, and his love.

A family is forever. A family unit may be eternal. We are busily engaged in declaring these truths worldwide today because we take literally the command to "go . . . and teach all nations." (Matthew 28:19.)

Strengthening the home must be done on a continuing basis in love and patience. The Lord has said, "Now I speak unto you concerning your families—if men will smite you, or your families, once, and ye bear it patiently and revile not against them, neither seek revenge, ye shall be rewarded; but if ye bear it not patiently, it shall be accounted unto you as being meted out as a just measure unto you. And again, if your enemy shall smite you the second time, and you revile not against your enemy, and bear it patiently, your reward shall be an hundredfold." (D&C 98:23-25.)

We must show constant love in laboring with all family members. Latter-day Saints do not give up on family members despite behavior or attitudes. The worth of the family is great in the eyes of the Lord.

How important are you in your own eyes? Do you treat yourself shabbily? Do you forget you are a temple of God? Or do you treat yourself as being one of great worth? Do you look upon yourself as though you were really a son or daughter of God? Do you have personal respect and honor for yourself? In all of these questions we need to realize that with God's help we can accomplish all things, and our potential is unlimited. What a blessing it is to us individually to know that if we walk in his paths we can merit security. God's joy is great when we repent and come back unto him. All that God has is available to his worthy children regardless of how long they have been away or lost.

Enjoy with me the soul-warming lesson of the prodigal son:

"A certain man had two sons: and the younger of them said to his father, Father, give me the portion of goods that falleth to me. And he divided unto them his living. And not many days after the younger son gathered all together, and took his journey into a far country, and there wasted his substance with riotous living. And when he had spent all, there arose a mighty famine in the land; and he began to be in want. And he went and joined himself to a citizen of that country; and he sent him into his fields to feed swine. And he would fain have filled his belly with the husks that the swine did eat: and no man gave unto him. And when he came to himself, he said, How many hired servants of my father's have bread enough and to spare, and I perish with hunger! I will arise and go to my father, and will say unto him, Father, I have sinned against heaven, and before thee, and am no more worthy to be called thy son: make me as one of thy hired servants. And he arose, and came to his father.

"But when he was yet a great way off, his father saw him, and had compassion, and ran, and fell on his neck, and kissed him. And the son said unto him, Father, I have sinned against heaven, and in thy sight, and am no more worthy to be called thy son. But the father said to his servants, Bring forth the best robe, and put it on him; and put a ring on his hand, and shoes on his feet: and bring hither the fatted calf, and kill it; and let us eat, and be merry: for this my son was dead, and is alive again; he was lost, and is found. And they began to be merry.

"Now his elder son was in the field: and as he came and drew nigh to the house, he heard musick and dancing. And he called one of the servants, and asked what these things meant. And he said unto him, Thy brother is come; and thy father hath killed the fatted calf, because he hath received him safe and sound. And he was angry, and would not go in: therefore came his father out, and intreated him. And he answering said to his father, Lo, these many years do I serve thee, neither transgressed I at any time thy commandment: and yet thou never gavest me a kid, that I might make merry with my friends: but as soon as this thy son was come, which hath devoured thy living with harlots, thou hast killed for him the fatted calf. And he said unto him, Son, thou art ever with me, and all that I have is thine. It was meet that we should make merry, and be glad: for this thy brother was dead, and is alive again; and was lost, and is found." (Luke 15:11-32.)

God loves us. We are of great worth in his sight. We must firmly resolve, "As for me and my house, we will serve the Lord." (Joshua 24:15.) If we do these things, we have been promised great joy and everlasting happiness.

"I Went Home"

Joseph Smith's home
is a worthy example
as we review
our daily priorities
and work
toward family perfection

When a small child is hurt, his feet automatically run toward home. Most of us want to share with those at home the joys of success and the pleasures of special events.

Not just children, but all of us will want to go home under joyous or trying circumstances as long as we find love, acceptance, security, and understanding there. Home should be the place in which a person can unburden his soul and find renewed strength to face the world; where there is comfort, joy, and understanding; where best friends live; and where we can learn to be our best selves.

Home should be an anchor, a port in a storm, a refuge, a happy place in which to dwell, a place where we are loved and where we can love. Home should be where life's greatest lessons are taught and learned. Home can be the center of one's earthly faith where love and mutual responsibility are appropriately blended.

After Joseph Smith had suffered the anguish and the excitement of one of the greatest visions in the history of all mankind, he tells us in his own words, "I went home." He turned to his home and family for strength and for sharing.

I would like to dwell on that significant declaration, "I went home." By examining the home to which Joseph turned, perhaps we can strengthen our own homes.

Joseph had startling news to share, an almost unbelievable experience, a situation bigger than he could handle alone. Past experience must have taught him that home is where problems can be solved and confidences and concerns shared. There he could relate his true feelings without fear or ridicule. As he "leaned up to the fireplace" in the warmth of his home, he shared the events of the day with his mother. She asked questions. She listened and, above all, she believed. She had provided this "soon-to-be prophet" with love, training, and a good home environment. His wonderful mother seemed to be the heart of the home. Thomas Jefferson said, "The happiness of the domestic fireplace is the first boon of heaven."

Ellen White shares these words: "The home should be to children the most attractive place in the world, and the mother's presence should be the greatest attraction." A noble mother helped prepare Joseph for the great work he was yet to perform. Oneness, common purpose, loyalty, fun, and proper example were some of the basic ingredients of strength found in the Smith home. Elton Trueblood understood well when he said, "The family is the only institution in our world where the kingdom of God can actually begin." A good mother is more than a pleasant memory; her love, teachings, and influence are building blocks for a strong person. Let me remind you of the basic characteristics found in the home to which Joseph turned in his greatest hour of need, and from which we can all learn.

The picture of Joseph Smith kneeling in the Sacred Grove is familiar to all of us. Around the world the results of that prayer have been felt. Have you ever wondered what inspired that young boy to turn to prayer when he was troubled and doubting?

Lucy, Joseph's mother, had planted the seeds. From an early age she depended on prayer for guidance and strength. When a beloved sister died, Lucy wrote, "The grief occasioned by the death of Lovina was preying upon my health and threatened my constitution with serious injury, and they hoped that to accompany my brother home might serve to divert my mind and thus prove a benefit to me. . . . In the midst of this anxiety of mind, I determined to obtain that which I had heard spoken so much of from the pulpit—a change of heart. To accomplish this I spent much of my time reading the Bible and praying." (Lucy Mack Smith, *History of Joseph Smith, by His Mother* [Bookcraft], pp. 30-31.)

Later in life Lucy was seriously troubled by the fact that she could not get her husband, Joseph Sr., to join with her in attending religious meetings. When all of her invitations and persuasion failed, she resorted to another measure. This was something she often did and of which her children were very much aware. She made her desires, anxieties, and frustrations known to her Heavenly Father in prayer. She writes: "*I retired to a grove not far distant,* where I prayed to the Lord in behalf of my husband—that the *true gospel* might be presented to him and that his heart might be softened so as to receive it, or that he might become more religiously inclined." (Ibid., p.43. Italics added.) When the gospel of Jesus Christ was restored, Joseph's father became a valiant member. He believed Joseph before he believed the gospel. The prayers of a mother were answered through the prayer of a son. If Lucy had not effectively taught that great family lesson, would Joseph have "retired to the grove"?

When Joseph was nine years old, his sister Sophronia, only ten, was near death with typhus fever. At this time Lucy Smith wrote these words: "In this moment of distraction my husband and myself clasped our hands, fell upon our knees by the bedside, and poured out our grief to God in prayer and supplication, beseeching him to spare our child yet a little longer. . . . From this time forward Sophronia continued mending, until she entirely recovered." (Ibid., pp. 52-53.) At an early age Joseph witnessed the humble faith of his parents and the healing powers of a loving God. A short time later his own faith and the faith of his family helped him endure the terrible pain when the operation on his leg took place.

Love of God and the unwavering knowledge of God's existence were part of Joseph's education in his home. These traits were not taught by lectures or scolding. Visual aids were ever present. Joseph saw his parents kneeling in prayer; he knew his mother went to a grove to petition the Lord; he felt the love of the Lord in his home. The family read the Bible, sang hymns, and discussed the scriptures together. Religious conduct was not a weekend activity. It was a way of daily life.

When President Spencer W. Kimball dedicated the Orem campus and buildings of the Utah Technical College, he said, "We should seek out honorable work, because work is an important dimension of life."

One summer two little boys spent many long hours putting together a homemade wagon.

Secondhand wheels were put on axles and nailed to a wooden box. A handle was laboriously fashioned and attached, and two coats of red paint applied. At last the wagon was finished and ready for use. As the boys looked with pride at their handiwork, one said to the other, "Which is more fun, making or having?" His friend considered the hours of work planning and the overcoming of problems and then replied, "Making is more fun, I guess."

A home that teaches the joy of making, the self-discipline of labor, the tenacity to finish, the blessing of teamwork will be the kind of home that will draw family members back to it.

These lessons were well taught in the Smith family. Money was scarce; land had to be cleared and homes built. A younger brother, William, was reported to have said all of this was "no lazy job." Joseph learned how to work as he labored side by side with family members on all kinds of projects.

This prophet-in-embryo was brought up in an atmosphere of love. Joseph knew the feeling of being cradled in his mother's arms when he was hurt or badly treated. He felt the love of brothers and sisters. He was especially close to his brother Hyrum. Their love for each other is well documented in Church history. Games and contests often filled leisure time, but bickering and fighting were not tolerated. Joseph Smith, Sr., had the love of his children. When they needed a listening ear or an understanding heart, he was available. "Under the tutelage of their father the family studied the scriptures together and were led by him in family prayer." (James B. Allen and Glen M. Leonard, *The Story of the Latter-day Saints* [Deseret Book, 1976], p.

21.) He practiced well the admonition, "Fathers, provoke not your children to wrath: but bring them up in the nurture and admonition of the Lord." (Ephesians 6:4.) The Bible was used to teach children to read and as a textbook when Joseph Smith, Sr., served as a teacher for children from nearby farms.

In the rugged, substantial homes built by the Smith family, more thought was given to affection than decoration. Now, as then, praise, reward, and recognition, a hug or a friendly pat on the back will bring children "back home" more quickly than crystal chandeliers, an oriental rug, or a new TV set. In an atmosphere of love and encouragement a child can become success oriented and learn what "I am a child of God" really means.

A model family is many things, but one thing it is not: it is not without problems. The way a family copes with its problems determines whether it is a model family or a problem family.

In his family Joseph learned to cope with problems. He learned to stand for what was right as he saw his parents stand firm when pressures would have made it easy to yield. Through the things that he suffered he gained strength. Pains endured during the operation on his leg were severe, but they were nothing compared with the hurts he received from slander, gossip, and lies. When neighbors and friends ridiculed him, he could always turn to his family and home for strength, support, and refuge.

In our homes today family members should be taught to face questionable statements and unreliable accusations with dignity and calmness. Correct points of view and accurate information should be taught. Parents and children can share and learn together as pertinent issues are discussed. Maturity and strength come when differences of opinion can be examined intelligently without panic or contention. Then family members will have the ability to face criticism without being intolerant or defensive.

If problem-solving can be a family affair, the door of home will be the first door a troubled family member will open when he is looking for help.

When Joseph Smith said "I went home," he gave all of us goals for which to strive. In his home he was nurtured and trained. He was understood. He was believed. Lucy's love, confidence, and trust in Joseph are perhaps best expressed in a few lines from the play *Joseph* by Ralph G. Rodgers, Jr., when Lucy Mack Smith said, "I believe my boy Joseph. I believe all that he told our family about his prayer to God, about his answer, his revelation. I believe him. Joseph never lied to me before, why should he lie to me now?"

Love, example, and correct teachings prepared him to face herculean tasks and severe trials.

New tasks and different trials are ever present. Let us look to our homes today. Do family members know they are loved? Do they find courage and strength in times of stress? Can they work hard? Do they finish jobs once begun? Is constant prayer a guide and comfort? Are the scriptures studied and the love of God understood? Is faith built? If so, from our homes will emerge people of faith, courage, wisdom, and action.

These people may in their turn establish homes with specifications similar to those of the Smith home, and possibly world problems will diminish.

The Smith family's home life is a worthy example to keep in front of us as we constantly review our daily priorities and work toward family perfection. Theodore F. Adams shares lofty observations in his "Beatitudes for the Home":

Blessed is the home where God is at home and where the spirit of Christ rules.

Blessed is the home where children are welcomed and given their rightful place.

Blessed is the home having a church home where father, mother, and children worship regularly together.

Blessed is the home where each puts the other's happiness first.

Blessed is the home where all show their love in ways that mean the most to those they love.

Blessed is the home where each seeks to bring out the best in each other and to show his own best self at all times.

Blessed is the home where all have learned to face their daily problems in a Christian spirit and to disagree without being disagreeable.

Blessed is the home where children grow up and grown-ups do not act like children.

Blessed is the home having the assurance of a heavenly home.

(*Words of Life* [New York: Harper and Row, 1966], p. 109.)

Let us examine our own homes and make improvements where improvements are needed. May God help us to make our homes places of quality where family members of all ages and circumstances can learn wisdom, solve their problems, and share their joys and concerns in a warm, friendly atmosphere. Then "I went home" will be not only a meaningful declaration, but will be a proper direction of life, earthly and eternally.

I bear you my witness that out of strong homes come strong people. God recognizes with pleasure families of one or more if they include Him and teach His ways. I declare these truths and bear my testimony that Joseph Smith is a prophet of God and a worthy product of a good home.

"This Is
No Harm"

Satan,
the father of lies,
tells us
"This is no harm"
and then lets us catch
ourselves
in our own snare

Not often do students remember for twenty-four hours very many words taught by their teachers. Yet fifty years later some former students recall with lasting appreciation the words one teacher had her class repeat at the beginning of each day. Every school morning this rather unpretentious, plain, wise woman implanted the meaning of honesty into our minds by having us recite, "A lie is any communication given to another with the intent to deceive."

When I compare this definition with that found in the dictionary, which states, "A lie is an untrue statement made with the intent of deceiving," I greatly appreciate her definition. A lie can be effectively communicated without words ever being spoken. Sometimes a nod of the head or silence can deceive. Recommending a questionable business investment, making a false entry in a ledger, devious use of flattery, or failure to divulge all pertinent facts are a few other ways to communicate the lie.

After having us go through this daily ritual, this wonderful teacher, who never married but who had such a motherly influence over many of us, would teach with few words the importance of communicating truth under all circumstances. Often she simply said, "Don't tell lies. Don't share lies. Don't participate in lies."

How serious is lying? We have a clue when we

read throughout the scriptures that Satan is the father of lies. His method of teaching this evil practice is illustrated in the tenth section of the Doctrine and Covenants: "Yea, he [Satan] saith unto them: Deceive and lie . . . behold, this is no harm. And thus he . . . telleth them that it is no sin to lie. . . . And thus he . . . causeth them to catch themselves in their own snare." (D&C 10:25-26.)

Yet we can't hide behind the father of lies and say, "Satan made me do it." All he does is tell us, "This is no harm," and then he lets us catch ourselves in our own snare.

It is a sin to lie. It is a tragedy to be the victim of lies. Being trapped in the snares of dishonesty and misrepresentation does not happen instantaneously. One little lie or dishonest act leads to another until the perpetrator is caught in the web of deceit. As Samuel Johnson wrote, "The chains of habit are generally too small to be felt until they are too strong to be broken." Those who become victims of this entrapment often struggle through life bearing their heavy burden because they are unwilling to acknowledge their problem and make the effort to change. Many are unwilling to pay the price to be free from the chains of lies. Some individuals may be very aware of the value of honesty and yet be unable to come up with the down payment.

Perhaps if we analyze some of the reasons people lie, we can avoid or overcome this vicious snare.

Sometimes we deceive and lie to avoid personal embarrassment. I recently heard of a young woman who had been released from her employment because of dishonesty. When she applied for another job, she told the prospective employer that her former boss had a family member he wanted to put in her place. She probably told her friends and family members the same story to avoid mortification.

Financial setbacks may be explained to others with untruths. Or have you ever heard someone say, "I was just too busy to get the job done," when, in truth, he had forgotten? Others use dishonesty to delay, to gain advantage, to impress, to flatter, or to destroy.

Consciously or unconsciously some people lie to destroy others. Jealousy or feelings of inferiority may cause us to degrade another's habits or character. Have you watched an overly ambitious person turn on false flattery for his own gain?

Lies are often excuses for lack of courage. Sometimes lies are nothing more than excuses for poor performance. Usually one lie or deception has to be covered by another. Lies cannot stand alone. Each one must continually be supported by more and more of its own kind.

There are some who would have us believe there is no right or wrong—that everything is relative. We must never allow ourselves to think that proper conduct and decision making are found in a convenient path somewhere between right and wrong.

In today's world where deceitfulness is so widely practiced in advertising, promoting, and marketing, a worthy prayer could well be, "Help me, O Lord, to be free not only of personal deceit, but grant me also the wisdom to avoid those who would damage me or mine through devious means."

How do we become victims of dishonesty?

There are many ways, but let me examine a few.

A potent statement from Isaiah sheds light on one reason: "Yea, they are greedy dogs which can never have enough, and they are shepherds that cannot understand: they all look to their own way, every one for his gain, from his quarter." (Isaiah 56:11.) Greed can make a person both dishonest and gullible. Such are spoken of in the Doctrine and Covenants. "Their eyes are full of greediness. These things ought not to be, and must be done away from among them." (D&C 68:31-32.) Good advice for those who would avoid deceitful propositions is found in section 9, verse 13: "Be faithful, and yield to no temptation."

A friend recently confided that he had lost heavily in a get-rich-quick scheme because he couldn't turn off his greed valve. Wanting more and more—living beyonds one's income—makes many persons susceptible to the dishonest promoter. The plan that offers exorbitant rewards or gives you—and only you—a once-in-a-lifetime deal is to be avoided.

Use of important, well-recognized names or undue reference to special community or religious affiliations is often used to gain confidence and open the door to sales deceptions.

Avoid those who want immediate decisions or cash right now. All worthwhile investment opportunities can bear deliberation and scrutiny. We must get all the available facts and consider them well, and then make decisions that are in the best interest of all. When marginal cases and situations arise, personal integrity must be an important element in any decision. When right actions are not clearly evident, personal honesty will lead us to discern and reveal relevant points or facts of which others may not be aware. A person of integrity will help others to be honest. A person of integrity will ask questions and give answers that are accurate. Integrity makes it possible for us to chart a course of righteous personal conduct long before the time for action arrives.

A wise person will not allow himself to be victimized by the unscrupulous because of false pride. Sometimes people are swindled because false pride prevents them from asking questions and seeking additional information. For fear of embarrassment or being thought ignorant, a prospect might nod his head in the affirmative when he really doesn't understand the glib salesman's line of chatter. "What does that mean?" "What are the risks?" "What are the pitfalls?" "What is the history of the company?" "What references do you have?"—these are questions worthy of pursuit. When promoters carelessly use simple but elusive words such as "hedge," "shelter," "exempt," "annuity," "umbrella," "tax free," "insulated," and "deferrable," the buyer had better be aware. Abraham Lincoln once said, "Stand with anybody that stands right. Stand with him while he is right and part with him when he goes wrong."

If prudent decisions cannot be reached on the basis of one's own expertise, advice should be sought from knowledgeable and trusted counselors. Offers that cannot wait or stand review are not worthy.

We are living in a day and time when the "gentle lie," the "soft lie," the "convenient lie," the "misleading lie," the "once-in-a-lifetime deal," the "opportunity for a few selected friends" are being vigorously advocated and promoted. Designing promoters of questionable schemes continue to prey on the gullible.

Fortunately, or unfortunately, the business climate is always good for those who have a deal to promote. In times of recession or depression, unwise debt is encouraged by promoters who would give us the opportunity to supplement our inadequate means. During periods of prosperity and plenty, some try to convince us that then is the time to borrow, speculate, and move up to higher levels of living by riding the waves of a guaranteed prosperous tomorrow. How often do we hear, "I would have made it big if the economy had not slowed down"? History should have taught all of us that there is enough risk and uncertainty in normal or conservative investments to cause the cautious to rebel at the exorbitant returns offered by those who would have us "bet on the come."

More often than not, those who can least afford to go into debt to provide funds for scheming money managers are those who are hurt the most when the day of final accounting arrives. It is true—getting into debt is a tanglesome web.

Samuel Johnson also said, "Do not accustom yourself to consider debt only as an inconvenience; you will find it a calamity." We encourage all to avoid going into debt for speculation purposes. "The love of money is the root of all evil." (1 Timothy 6:10.) A proper balance in our money management skills should be the continuing goal of all who would be free of financial bondage.

President N. Eldon Tanner wisely suggests, "The choice to serve God, worthily made, does not necessarily preclude a home or sufficient money or income, or the things of this world which bring joy and happiness, but it does require that we must *not* turn away from God and the teachings of Jesus Christ while in the pursuit of our temporal needs." (*Ensign*, June 1971, p. 14.)

It should be the goal of every Latter-day Saint to become the kind of person of whom it can be said, "His word is his bond." In all of our words and deeds we should ask ourselves, "Is it right? Is it true?" not "Is it expedient, satisfactory, convenient, or profitable?" just, "Is it right?" The wise will consider, "What is right?"; the greedy, "What will it pay?"

Sometimes investment promoters, because of the pressures of pending financial reverses and tragedy, scramble and use devious delay tactics while they struggle for survival. Honesty will be compromised by some when failure lurks. People with integrity will stand true and firm in success or disaster.

Honesty is basic. It is true that lying is an accomplice to every other form of vice. Or, as Oliver Wendell Holmes has said, "Sin has many tools, but a lie is the handle which fits them all." Lying damages others. Lying subtly permits us to destroy ourselves as we are caught in the snare and shatter our own self-image and credibility. Freedom from deceit and lying improves self and gives all of us peace of mind.

Not long ago a troubled friend of mine who has long suffered and continues to suffer the pains of a victim entrapped in his own snare of lies said, "I have been living lies for so long and have told so many over the years that, frankly, I don't really know when I am telling the truth." When I first heard this, I was moved with compassion; but a second thought had me wondering if this, too, wasn't just another lie. Lying has filled this friend's life full of trouble. No one will ever convince this victim of deceit that "this is no harm."

He who lies is the servant of the lie. He who tells the lie must live with the results. Deacons and Beehive girls should be taught the evils of deceit. Teachers and Mia Maids should be taught the importance of truth. Priests and Laurels should be taught the pitfalls that accompany dishonesty. Missionaries, to be successful and happy, must live by correct principles. Primary children can learn that telling lies is not good. Children are entitled to see honesty taught by example in the home. Unfortunate is the individual or family who is taught that honesty is a policy rather than the proper way of life.

We live in a world of law. We may be able to avoid or skirt laws of the land, but the laws of heaven have an irrevocable effect on us today, tomorrow, and forever. "Ye shall know the truth, and the truth shall make you free." (John 8:32.) No man will ever be totally free who is living a lie. Only he who bears or who has borne such a continuing burden can relate appropriately to such a declaration. We should ever bear in mind that a wrong isn't right just because many people do it. A wrong deed isn't right just because it hasn't become visible.

May our Heavenly Father help us to have the courage to acknowledge and cast aside the living of a lie or the perpetuation of lies. Honesty is more than a policy. It is a happy way of life as we deal with our fellowmen, and particularly as we live with ourselves.

Whether we are like the good schoolteacher mentioned in the beginning of this chapter, or a friend, neighbor, or family member, let us live and teach honesty. In the academic classroom and in the classroom of life, the virtues of honesty should be stressed by all who espouse the principle that "the glory of God is intelligence, or, in other words, light and truth." (D&C 93:36.) Light and truth will help us to forsake the evil one and come off victorious. "This is no harm" is the declaration of our mortal enemy. He would lead us to self-destruction.

If a lie is any communication given to another with the intent to deceive, we will all do well to seek God's constant help in understanding and finding the truth. People of integrity will neither foster, nourish, embrace, nor share the lie. People of wisdom will not let greed, fear, or the desire for quick riches lead them into the snares of the dishonest and unscrupulous who prey on the gullible in order to maneuver from them valuable possessions.

May we constantly remind ourselves to "seek not for riches but for wisdom; and, behold, the mysteries of God shall be unfolded unto you, and then shall you be made rich. Behold, he that hath eternal life is rich." (D&C 11:7.)

Who
Will Forfeit
the Harvest?

How to avoid
the stony places:
unwillingness
to accept human qualities,
to accept change,
to follow instructions,
to be totally
committed

Today in many places of the world it is harvest time. Crops are being gathered for the use and benefit of all mankind. Besides being an appropriate time for all of us to give thanks, harvest time should be a time of personal contemplation, evaluation, and planning. In farming or in just plain living, what contributes to a successful harvest? What can we do to ensure better crops and production? On the other hand, what could cause us to forfeit the harvest?

In the thirteenth chapter of Matthew, by use of the parable of the sower, the Savior points out conditions that cause crop failure. He answers the question, "Who will forfeit the harvest?" His warnings and observations are worthy. The same stony places are with us now; and unless we are mindful, our personal harvest can be lost.

"Behold, a sower went forth to sow; and when he sowed, some seeds fell by the way side, and the fowls came and devoured them up: Some fell upon stony places, where they had not much earth; and forthwith they sprung up, because they had no deepness of earth: And when the sun was up, they were scorched; and because they had no root, they withered away. . . .

"But he that received seed unto the good ground is he that heareth the word, and understandeth it; which also beareth fruit, and bringeth forth, some an hundredfold, some sixty, some thirty." (Matthew 13:3-6, 23.)

The promise of the harvest is there for those who receive the seed unto good ground and establish roots that are strong.

Let me share with you four prevalent conditions on the horizon today that can cause us to lose the harvest.

1. *Unwillingness to accept human qualities.* When Jesus had taught with such profound wisdom, judgment, and skill, some of those closest to him were astonished by his amazing abilities and miracles and asked, "Whence hath this man this wisdom, and these mighty works? Is not this the carpenter's son? is not his mother called Mary? and his brethren . . . and his sisters, are they not all with us?" (Matthew 13:54-56.) They were mightily impressed, even astonished, at his words and works, but they had difficulty accepting the source.

Today some are sowing seeds on stony places because they, too, doubt the authority of those who give counsel and direction. There is a tendency on the part of some to ignore, criticize, or rebel because they cannot accept the *human* delivery system. Some will not accept Jesus Christ as the Savior because they are waiting for a Prince of Peace to come who is not quite as human as Jesus of Nazareth. Questions such as, "Is not this the carpenter's son?" "Is not this the one born in a manger?" "Can there any good thing come out of Nazareth?" (John 1:46)—these are evidences of the weaknesses of men who are unwilling to accept the human qualities of those who are called and raised up to give direction and counsel.

We, too, should not be deceived by doubters who would use the same tactics by planting thorns to destroy the harvest. How can we avoid crop failure in this area of concern? By not allowing our roots to be withered away by winds and storms of questions such as these: "Is not this the one who was raised in Arizona?" "Is not this the one who came from Canada?" "Is not this the one who was born in Mexico?" "Go to our new bishop for counsel? Is not he the one who lives just up the street?"

We read in Matthew: "And they were offended in him. But Jesus said unto them, A prophet is not without honour, save in his own country, and in his own house. And he did *not* many mighty works there because of their unbelief." (Matthew 13:57-58. Italics added.)

The concept that "a prophet is not without honour, save in his own country, and in his own house" was a tragedy for these Galilean people. Shortly after this time Jesus left Nazareth and the Galilean ministry to concentrate most of his efforts in the southern part of the country nearer Jerusalem. Think of what miracles, manifestations, and healings of body and soul might have been enjoyed by these people if their faith had been sufficient to accept the great works of his faith.

Sadly enough, I think we see this around us now. Someone who daily walks and talks and enjoys the presence of a Joseph Smith or a Spencer W. Kimball, but who is still essentially without faith, may have great difficulty in accepting them as prophets. I remember President Harold B. Lee telling the story of a very prominent man from New

York who could not accept Joseph Smith as a prophet because he was "too close to home."

Will we forfeit the harvest because we cannot accept direction, revelation, or counsel from someone who just lives down the street, in the ward, or in the stake? Will we reject leadership from the churchman who is human, with frailties, and who has family members who may be quite human also?

While we are struggling with an "Is-not-this-the-carpenter's-son?" attitude, we may be missing the truth, the way, and the ultimate harvest. Jesus was not accepted as the Only Begotten Son of God by thousands who preferred to recognize him as "just the child of Mary."

The worth and significance of a President Joseph Fielding Smith, Brigham Young, or Joseph Smith is not measured by his physical stature, wearing apparel, or public image. Whether eternal truths were taught by one who dwelled near the Sea of Galilee or by one who lived in upstate New York, the size, origin, image, or popularity of the teachers cannot detract from the value of the truths they shared.

Safety can be assured for us if we "believe all that God has revealed, all that He does now reveal, and . . . that He will yet reveal many great and important things pertaining to the Kingdom of God." (Article of Faith 9.) May I add that these revelations will come through people—even the prophets with human qualities.

2. *Unwillingness to accept change.* If we are unable to accept change, in the language of the parable of the sower, we are those with no root. "Yet hath he not root in himself, but dureth for a while: for when

tribulation or persecution ariseth because of the word, by and by he is offended." (Matthew 13:21.)

If our roots are deep, we will welcome continuing revelation, change, and direction. We will develop the ability to accept releases, callings, and new challenges with enthusiasm. We will be too busy to be offended. We will be too big to be hurt. We will serve wherever we are called with anxious dedication. We will accept people for what they are and what they can and do become. Change will not only drive our roots deeper, but will also cause them to grow into new and fertile soil.

Some years ago a young mother of my acquaintance shared this event in her life. She had been active in youth programs in the ward for several years and was at the time president of the young women. The stake president called one day and asked her to meet with the stake presidency the following Sunday afternoon. With anxiety in her voice and tears close to the surface, she went to her husband and said, "I'm afraid they want me for a stake job. I don't want a stake job. I love the ward. I love the youth in the ward. I love my counselors. I love my job. I don't want to change." Her husband said, "Please go and see what they want. I'll support you in any assignment."

Her fears were realized. She was asked to be stake president of the Young Women. Later, the stake president told her that after she had reluctantly accepted the call, he had never seen a more forlorn-looking person walk out of his office.

For over six years, she, with the same sisters as counselors, took care of the stake work for the Young Women. "Those were some of the best years of service for me," she said. "My horizons expanded. I became acquainted with the wonderful leaders and great young people in our stake. I even had leadership experiences with other fine leaders in the whole valley. Later the opportunity came to serve on a general board. I shudder to think what I would have missed if I had declined the change in assignments."

Our Father in heaven knows what we need. Change is difficult. Change can be fearful. But change in the right direction is a growing process. Each new assignment, each new experience in the gospel framework, if fulfilled to the best of one's ability, adds new strengths.

Resistance to and resentment of change, of new assignments, of new opportunities are stony places that may keep our roots in the gospel from going deep and growing strong.

It was Theodore I. Rubin who wisely said, "If we let it, life produces endless experiences that demand change. If you are motivated and willing to struggle, you can change and grow for as long as you live. This is the challenge, the pain, and the joy of being human."

Sometimes we are unwise and even cruel in our unwillingness to accept change in others. I recently learned of a man who raised his family and pursued his professional life in a small country town. He was not without his problems, but was a good man with a great heart who loved the Lord and the gospel. Mistakes, even small ones, are not soon forgotten in some neighborhoods, however; and he never seemed to be "allowed" to grow, blossom, develop, and change into what he could become.

As a missionary serving overseas, he had made a

remarkable contribution. The mission president said he had done more to bridge the cultural gap between the two countries than any other adult American was able to do. When his mission was over, he returned to the small town, and there, without malice or evil intent but with the insistent burden of memory, his neighbors did not invite him or let him be the man he had become, but rather seemed quite prepared to see him as the less attractive man of an earlier period. Because of their expectations, he completed the last years of his life much less happy and much less involved and surely much less productive to the kingdom than he had been for that one glorious period where people in a new land and in a different time allowed him to change and to be what he really wanted to be and, in his heart, really was.

Let me share one other example. A friend of mine went to school with a boy who did not have much home life and for whom the gospel did not mean as much as it later would. He drank a little and caroused a little; but later, after moving away from his home town, he became very active in the Church. His one dream was to return to his hometown and start a business, which he tried to do. But unfortunately, as with the other man, the people in the community insisted on treating him as he had been, not as what he had become. He finally moved away and is doing remarkably well in business and in the Church. He recently expressed to my friend how deeply disappointed he was that his former friends and townspeople had not let him "come home," even in a gospel sense.

3. *Unwillingness to follow instructions.* These are they who may forfeit the harvest because they will not be obedient. "Hearing they hear not, neither do they understand" is the description the parable of the sower uses to describe those who fall into this vulnerable territory. (Matthew 13:13.) "And some fell among thorns; and the thorns sprung up, and choked them." (Matthew 13:7.) We, too, will fall among the thorns and be led away from our promised blessings if we fail in obedience.

I was very impressed when I heard an eager, reactivated elder say, "I'm back in the Church and active today because my elders quorum president came to see me when I didn't want to be seen, and loved me when I didn't want to be loved." Here is an elders quorum president obediently doing his job as it should be done.

Sometimes when we are asked to be obedient, we do not know why, except that the Lord has commanded. From 1 Nephi 9:5 we read, "Wherefore, the Lord hath commanded me to make these plates for a wise purpose in him, which purpose I know not." Nephi followed instructions even though he didn't fully understand the wise purpose. His obedience resulted in blessings to mankind all over the world. By not obeying our present-day leaders, we plant our seeds in stony places and may forfeit the harvest.

4. *Unwillingness to be totally committed.* The parable of the sower would refer to these as those who have no deepness. They are those without commitment or testimony. These are those who would be convenience members. Some testimonies spring up

quickly and flourish for a while until the heat comes
on or a stony place is encountered. Then the wither-
ing starts to take place.

"Some fell upon stony places, where they had
not much earth: and forthwith they sprung up, because they had no *deepness* of earth." (Matthew 13:5.
Italics added.)

Deep and enduring testimonies grow and
strengthen as they are daily nurtured. They increase
as they are shared. Meaningful testimonies have
roots planted in fertile soil. The sun, the rain, and
even the storms make them stronger and more dur-
able. As the events of daily life come upon us, some
testimonies wither under the heat of everyday
occurrences. Roots are shallow, testimonies fade,
and there is no harvest.

Let us seek to be totally committed. Then we
will not fall upon stony places, wither away, or stray
from the paths of security and happiness. Those
who serve with complete dedication wherever they
are called do not wilt, wither, wonder, or wander.
Their roots are deep and solidly planted in the fertile soils of the kingdom. The harvest is enjoyed with
every passing day as they serve.

Let us not forfeit the harvest. If we forfeit the
harvest, what do we lose? We lose day by day pleasures of growth and development that come from
doing our tasks in the framework of the gospel. We
lose the satisfaction of accomplishing difficult tasks
and serving better.

Most of all, we forfeit the gift of eternal growth
and progress. May we avoid the stony places of (1)
unwillingness to accept human qualities, (2) unwillingness to accept change, (3) unwillingness to

follow instructions, (4) unwillingness to be totally committed. By so doing we can establish deep, strong roots and thus reap the harvest our Father in heaven wants for all his children.

Progress
through Change

There is pain
in change,
but there is also
great satisfaction
in recognizing
that progress
is being achieved

When a choice plant became rootbound and began to deteriorate, a young friend of ours decided to transplant it to a larger container. Carefully he lifted the greenery from its small pot and put it into its larger home, trying to disturb the roots and soil as little as possible. The novice gardener watched and waited. To his dismay, the plant still struggled. Our friend expressed his frustration to an experienced gardener, who offered his services. When the plant was placed in the gardener's hands, he turned the pot upside down, pulled out the plant, shook the soil from the roots, and clipped and pulled all the stragglers from the root system. Replacing the plant into the pot, he vigorously pushed the soil tightly around the plant. Soon the plant took on new life and grew.

How often in life do we set our own roots into the soil of life and become rootbound? We may treat ourselves too gently and defy anyone to disturb the soil or trim back our root system. Under these conditions we too must struggle to make progress. Oh, change is hard! Change can be rough.

The Lord does not want His church to become rootbound and stagnant. Constant revelation through the prophets is needed for the growth of His kingdom.

There is nothing so unchanging, so inevitable as change itself. The things we see, touch, and feel are always changing. Relationships between friends, husband and wife, father and son, brother and sister are all dynamic, changing relationships. There is a constant that allows us to use change for our own good, and that constant is the revealed eternal truths of our Heavenly Father.

We need not feel that we must forever be what we presently are. There is a tendency to think of change as the enemy. Many of us suspect change and will often fight and resist it before we have even discovered what the actual effects will be. When change is thought through carefully, it can produce the most rewarding and profound experiences in life. The changes we make must fit the Lord's purposes and patterns.

As opportunity for change reaches into our lives, as it always will, we must ask, "Where do I need development? What do I want out of life? Where do I want to go? How can I get there?" Weighing alternatives very carefully is a much needed prerequisite as one plans changes. In God's plan we are usually free to choose the changes we make in our lives and we are always free to choose how we will respond to the changes that come. We need not surrender our freedoms. But just as a compass is valuable to guide us out of the dense forest, so the gospel points the way as we walk the paths of life.

C. S. Lewis indicated there is often pain in change when he wrote of God's expectations for His children: "Imagine yourself as a living house. God comes in to rebuild that house. At first, perhaps, you can understand what He is doing. He is getting the drains right and stopping the leaks in the roof and so on: you knew that those jobs needed doing and so you are not surprised. But presently He starts knocking the house about in a way that hurts abominably and does not seem to make sense. What on earth is He up to? The explanation is that He is building quite a different house from the one you thought of—throwing out a new wing here, putting on an extra floor there, running up towers, making courtyards. You thought you were going to be made into a decent little cottage: but He is building a palace." (C. S. Lewis, *Mere Christianity* [New York: Macmillan Co., 1960], p. 174.)

Yes, there is pain in change, but there is also great satisfaction in recognizing that progress is being achieved. Life is a series of hills and valleys, and often the best growth comes in the valleys. Change is a meaningful part of repentance. Some are unable to repent because they are unwilling to change.

Some time ago I was participating in a groundbreaking ceremony for a chapel at the Utah State Prison. After the ceremonies, Warden Morris invited Governor Scott Matheson and me to take a tour of the facilities. We had noticed the extra care that had been taken to make the grounds around the maximum-security building pleasing and beautiful. When we asked the warden who had done the work, he indicated that two inmates had been given time outside of their cells to improve the landscape. We asked if we could meet the two men. The warden took us into the maximum facility to see them. As Marvel and Brown shuffled toward us from their restricted confinements on death row, we felt that the look on their faces reflected their unspoken question, "What have we done wrong now?"

"We want to compliment you men on the work

you have done on the grounds," we said. "The flower beds and vegetable gardens look beautiful and well kept. Congratulations on your good work."

The change that came over their expressions was marvelous. The unexpected words of praise had given them reason for self-esteem. Someone had noticed that their efforts had changed a rocky, weed-filled yard into a beautiful garden. Sadly, they had failed earlier to make productive gardens out of the rocky, weed-covered fields of their own lives. But we hold hope for men like these who could see a need for change in one area and had accomplished much good. Perhaps their part in changing the gardens will lead to improvement in their own lives.

Philosopher William James once said, "The greatest discovery of my generation is that we *can* change our circumstances by changing our attitudes of mind." Jesus Christ helped people from all walks of life reach heights they had never dreamed of by teaching them to walk in new, secure paths.

Many begin their lives in such dire and adverse circumstances that change seems impossible. Let me share with you some examples of impossible beginnings.

The first example is a child who had an extremely unhappy home life. His family moved from one state to another until he was eight years of age. He was often beaten by his father, who was either too strict or not strict enough, according to his mood at the time. The boy spent many of his early years sleeping in buses, train stations, and cheap hotels. At the age of fourteen he was arrested as a runaway. Both family and friends classified him as untrustworthy, often violent, and a loner.

The second example is a boy who was frail at

birth. Throughout his childhood he had a tendency toward infection. His frail body seemed unable to hold his oversized head. His father worried that people considered his son "addled," and on one occasion he beat the boy publicly. After his mother had lost three previous children, she wrapped herself in black and withdrew from society.

In the third instance, a young man came from circumstances of near poverty. His family was forced to move more than once because of financial difficulties. He had little, if any, formal schooling. His mother reported that "he was less inclined to read and study than any of the other children." Because neighbors considered many of his ways and ideas strange, he was ostracized by his peers. All his life he was hounded by the law and found himself constantly in difficulty.

Certain steps can help one make constructive, worthwhile changes in life. "When you climb up a ladder, you must begin at the bottom, and ascend step by step, until you arrive at the top, and so it is with the principles of the gospel." (*History of the Church* 6:306-7.) In order to make significant changes in our lives, we must accept our Father in heaven and His truths. The prophet Alma in the Book of Mormon said, "Have ye spiritually been born of God? Have ye received his image in your countenances? Have ye experienced this mighty change in your hearts?" (Alma 5:14.)

Let me suggest four important steps in making change a valuable tool in our lives:

First, we must understand the need for change. An unexamined life is not worth living. A new bishop shared with me an experience that frustrated him. A young lady in his ward was not living as she should. When he counseled her, she bristled and said that he should be willing to accept her the way she was. She would not accept the fact that "the way she was" was just not good enough for her bishop, for her Heavenly Father, and, most important, for herself. Being aware of the fault and the need to change is a most important step. *Recognition of the need to change has to be a greater force than the luxury of staying the same.*

Second, the facts must be authentic. We need to know how, what, where, and why to change. The gospel of Jesus Christ can help us set short-term, intermediate, and long-term goals by teaching us who we are, where we came from, why we are here, and where we are going. With this knowledge, a person will have greater strength to improve.

Third, a system for change must be established. It was Emerson who said, "A man who sits on the cushion of advantage goes to sleep. When he is pushed, tormented, defeated, he puts on his wits, learns moderation and real skills." Our change must be planned and orderly. After our system for change is established, it must be followed through to completion, even though it may disturb our very root system.

Fourth, we must be totally committed to our plan for change. A Chinese proverb says, "Great souls have wills; feeble souls have only wishes." Unless we have the will to improve, all the other steps to change will be wasted. This last step separates the winners from the losers.

Earlier I mentioned three examples of people living in the most dire circumstances. The first young man's life was a series of continuing arrests for everything from vagrancy to armed robbery and murder. Never recognizing the need to change, he was one day convicted of murder.

The second was a description of the early years of Thomas A. Edison. From a beginning that seemed almost too much to overcome, he was able to change and build. Though he was once judged retarded, he proved himself to be one of the greatest inventors of all time. His personal commitment changed the whole world for the better.

The third tells the story of a young man and his early days in the northeastern part of this country. He was born in 1805 during a hard, cold Vermont winter. His name—Joseph Smith. His beginnings were difficult. Life was a series of struggles, not only physically, but also emotionally and spiritually. But here was a young man who recognized the need for improvement through change and who submitted to authority greater than himself. From tremendously difficult beginnings, he sought change and ushered in the last dispensation. His faith, prayers, and works brought to the earth the greatest, most profound changes in the latter days.

It has been said by Bruce Barton that "when we're through changing, we're through." There is no age when we are too old or too young or just too middle-aged to change. Perhaps old age really comes when a person finally gives up the right, challenge, and joy of changing. We should remain teachable. How easy it is to become set. We must be willing to establish goals whether we are sixty, seventy, fifty, or fifteen. We must maintain a zest for life. Never should there be a time when we are unwilling to improve ourselves through meaningful change.

For many Church members it is often difficult to accept change in leadership. On ward and stake levels leadership changes are necessary and, oftentimes, too frequent for our convenience and comfort. Some of us are inclined to resent and resist personnel changes. "Why can't they leave him in?" or "Why do we have to have her?" or "Why do they have to divide our ward?" Our vision may be limited. Seldom are changes made that do not bring needed progress to a person or a situation. How often in retrospect have we thought, "I didn't understand why that change was made in the program or why that person was given such a calling, but now I can see that it was just what was needed for the time."

During transitional times—and there are always transitional times in the Church—patience, love, and long-suffering are needed. A permanent part of our philosophy should be, "Never allow yourself to be offended by someone who is learning his job."

Change in our own church assignments may be even more disturbing. Often when we express a wish to never have *that* assignment, the bishop or stake president offers us the blessings of that self-same calling. At those times it is good to remember the words of Paul, who, though he was troubled by many ailments, said, "I can do all things through Christ which strengtheneth me." (Philippians 4:13.)

For us as a church with lay leadership, the blessings of change come often. Very few of us feel adequate to meet those changes with our own talents.

How grateful we can be for the strength of Jesus Christ, which helps us with the changes brought by new callings and increased responsibilities.

The change from this life to a life with Him who is our Eternal Father is the ultimate goal to which meaningful change can bring us. May we all seek and accept wholesome, orderly changes for the betterment of our personal lives.

Roadblocks
to Progress

Many of us
set up roadblocks
to progress
and contribute
to our own unhappiness
while we wait
for others
to seek us out
and offer help

An unhappy mother, who had been left alone to care for herself and her three young children, indicated that she was not attending church anymore. "Why should I? I have lived in the same apartment now for more than four months, and not one person has come to call on us."

She seemed taken back and surprised when, instead of saying, "I will have the bishop contact you promptly," I asked, "How many people have you visited since you moved into your new neighborhood?"

Many of us set up roadblocks to progress and contribute to our own unhappiness while we wait for others to seek us out and offer help. Negative attitudes lived with today cause stagnation, misery, and bitterness tomorrow. It is unproductive for those who should be anxiously engaged in seeking the abundant life to nurse personal hurts. We are all God's children. If we love Him, we will feed His sheep wherever they may be found, without regard to our own personal plight or situation. Often we can best feed others when we are hungry ourselves or not completely comfortable in the fold that we presently occupy. Often those who are hungry, helpless, and cold can best be rescued by those who have been through the same exposures. Marking time or stalling should not be indulged in by the weak, weary, uncertain, and unrecognized. Instead, there is a healing power as we use our energy in action, in service, and in lifting others.

It was Booker T. Washington who wisely stated, "Success is to be measured not so much by the position that one has reached in life as by the obstacles which he has overcome while trying to succeed." Victories in life come through our ability to work around and over the obstacles that cross our path. We grow stronger as we climb our own mountains.

"The brightest crowns that are worn in heaven have been tried, and smelted, polished and glorified through the furnace of tribulation," according to Thomas Carlyle.

Let me share four basic contributing factors that might prevent our personal progress and church activity: (1) the constant nursing of personal hurts, (2) yielding to the sorrow of tragedy and grief, (3) being fettered with the habits and mistakes of misconduct, (4) letting fears inhibit progress. Let us ponder these enemies of eternal progress and seek to gather the courage to cast them aside.

1. *The constant nursing of personal hurts.* Each of us should daily resolve that with God's help we will not allow careless words from others to shape our destiny or control our daily course. How tragic it is to see, on occasion, a life of usefulness lost because someone has allowed an unkind comment to cause a wound or hurt. The person lets the injury become an open sore and fester rather than treating it with prompt skill and maturity. Some try to get even with their offenders by dropping out of life's race. How weak, how damaging, how self-restricting is the often-used statement, "I'll never go back as long as

that person is there!" On occasion some of us seem to stand on the sidelines waiting to be hurt, offended, or ignored. We listen for careless words from others, remember the unsaid hellos, and read into the said or unsaid words a totally unintended message.

One of the finest basketball players of all time was asked what had contributed the most to his outstanding success. His answer was, "I learned to play in pain. Although injuries, bruises, and bumps came, I never allowed myself the luxury of slowing down or quitting."

The greatest teacher and leader also showed the world an example of proper conduct when He was the victim of unkind words and cruel deeds. He simply said, "Father, forgive them; for they know not what they do." (Luke 23:34.)

During his earthly mission Jesus made every confrontation a learning experience, including those that would be destructive or cause hurt and dissatisfaction. He was never rebellious, never ashamed; always long-suffering, patient, kingly; and never deterred in being about His Father's business. He, too, proved His greatness when His personal pain and suffering were the most intense. Hurting words and unkind deeds never kept Him from reaching His goals. No one can meet life in all its fulness without experiencing hurt, pain, and suffering.

The wise person will avoid the flood of bitterness and hatred that can be caused by the waters of hurt. He will constantly pursue the Savior's paths without stopping at this roadblock caused by apparent or real injustices. It is up to us to go forward and not confuse or confound ourselves. Those of us who cannot forgive and forget break the bridges over which we must pass. Too often we allow incidents to contribute to our stagnation when we permit ourselves to feel ignored, unwanted, or unworthy. How damaging sympathy is when it is self-administered! How refreshing it is to meet people who don't have time to be offended! Certainly what we are is more important than what we have or what is said of us.

2. *Yielding to the sorrow of tragedy and grief.* Too often the tragic loss of a child, husband, wife, mother, father, or other loved one becomes a turning point in life. Some yield to the damaging thought that if there be an all-wise and loving Eternal Father, how could He allow this to happen to me and mine? We allow the heartache to break the band and strengthening tie to Him who has promised to see us successfully through our Gethsemanes. Some of us in our moments of greatest despair turn away in bitterness from the arm of strength, comfort, and peace. Sometimes in our darkest hours we lose sight of the light as we dwell upon the unanswerable questions: "Why does God permit this to happen to me or to our family? What have we done to deserve this?"

This incident was shared by Lucile F. Johnson of Orem, Utah. "There was an attractive lady whose company everyone sought and enjoyed. She was a delight to be around because she seemed to love life and people to the fullest. One day I said to her, 'You are such a joy to all of us. What is your secret? Can you tell me?'

"'Yes,' she answered. 'One word changed my life.'

"'And what was that word?' I queried.

"'Malignant!' Startled, I heard this explanation:

'The doctor said that word to me and told me I had a limited time to live. I had a choice. I could make everyone miserable or I could try to make others happy. On my knees I realized that I had one day at a time just as everyone else has. I was able to see things I had never seen. My husband, my children, each person took on a beauty you can't believe. I know that life is a gift whether it be a day or a year, and I intend to enjoy my gift to the maximum.'"

Whether the works of God are manifest in healings or in the exhibition of courage and acceptance by those challenged must be left to the ultimate wisdom of Him who comprehendeth all things. How refreshing and strengthening are the lives of those who push upward and onward despite tragedies and griefs.

Edna Wheeler Wilcox has expressed this in her poem "The Winds of Fate."

> *One ship drives east and another drives west*
> *With the selfsame winds that blow.*
> *'Tis the set of the sails*
> *And not the gales*
> *Which tells us the way to go.*
>
> *Like the winds of the sea are the ways of fate,*
> *As we voyage along through life;*
> *'Tis the set of a soul*
> *That decides its goal,*
> *And not the calm or the strife.*

3. *Being fettered with habits and mistakes of misconduct.* A friend of mine who in recent months has made giant steps toward purposeful living and com-

plete activity in the Church shared the following: "I can tell you as one who has had many years of experience and practice that it is much easier to criticize individuals and knock the establishment than it is to change oneself and recognize the real causes for one's own inactivity and negativism."

Change is hard. Rather than going through the struggle to overcome a bad habit or rectify a mistake, some of us choose to make excuses for inactivity. Progress comes as we are able to give up something for something we want more. Honesty with oneself and setting of desirable but attainable goals day by day can determine the paths we follow. One might make a list of goals and then a price list for each goal. One day at a time the price of change can be paid. The cost will then not be overwhelming.

The Lord has promised that He will forgive and remember no more when the process of repentance is complete. If the Lord will do that for us, why should we not so do for ourselves? Mistakes can be forgiven. Habits can be changed. One more roadblock to progress can be removed.

In contrast to this process, how discouraging it is to witness someone who lives with damaging habits and who resists taking personal steps toward better self-management. William James said, "That which holds the attention determines the action." The truly repentant will put their mistakes behind, learn from them, and turn their attention from them to actions that bring progress and growth. How comforting it is to know that God will take us by the hand and lift us to new levels of attitude and achievement if we will but let Him. What a sweet, personal victory it is to recognize misdirection in one's own life and pay the price that then lets us walk in His paths.

4. *Letting fears inhibit progress.* Fear is another roadblock that may stop our eternal progress. It keeps us from attempting anything significant because we are afraid of failure or rejection. We won't accept opportunities for service in the Church or in the community because we might make a mistake.

"For God hath not given us the spirit of fear; but of power, and of love, and of a sound mind." (2 Timothy 1:7.) What a tragedy it is in our lives when we are afraid to try, afraid to make decisions, afraid to trust the Lord, or even afraid to make an error in judgment. Oh, that we could remember the great teaching of the Savior to Peter when fear caused him to fail to walk and even to sink:

"But the ship was now in the midst of the sea, tossed with waves: for the wind was contrary. And in the fourth watch of the night Jesus went unto them, walking on the sea. And when the disciples saw him walking on the sea, they were troubled, saying, It is a spirit; and they cried out for fear. But straightway Jesus spake unto them, saying, Be of good cheer; it is I; be not afraid.

"And Peter answered him and said, Lord, if it be thou, bid me come unto thee on the water.

"And he said, Come. And when Peter was come down out of the ship, he walked on the water, to go to Jesus. But when he saw the wind boisterous, he was afraid; and beginning to sink, he cried, saying, Lord, save me. And immediately Jesus stretched forth his hand, and caught him, and said unto him, O thou of little faith, wherefore didst thou doubt?" (Matthew 14:24-31.)

Fears in our lives can be conquered if we will but have faith and move forward with purpose. The constant nursing of personal hurts is a crutch for those who would move with hesitation, if at all. Yielding to the pains of tragedy and grief deters self-development and takes away the opportunity for triumph over trying obstacles. Being fettered with habits and mistakes of misconduct relegates a person to being a victim of his errors. Letting fears inhibit progress is but another evidence of one's unwillingness to try because of the fear of failure. Roadblocks to eternal progress are cast aside when resolves are made that no man needs to walk alone. It is a happy day when we come to know that with God's help nothing is impossible for us.

Adversity and You

We become
God's disciples when
we continue faithfully
under all circumstances,
including suffering
and tragedy

The other day I enjoyed listening to two of my friends discuss their favorite football team. They were in agreement that possibly the greatest limiting factor in the team's achieving high national ranking was its game schedules. They felt the team, for its own good, should play against stronger competition.

In football or in life, the adversaries—the ones with whom we compete or whom we oppose or resist, our opponents, our foes, our enemies, or our problems—are often the determining factors in our ultimate strength and achievement.

Adversity will surface in some form in every life. How we prepare for it, how we meet it, makes the difference. We can be broken by adversity, or we can become stronger. The final result is up to the individual. Henry Fielding said: "Adversity is the trial of principle. Without it, a man hardly knows whether he is honest or not."

Realizing that adversity can include suffering, destitution, affliction, calamity, or disaster, how can we best use it as an opportunity for personal growth and development? For one answer, let me share with you an incident in the life of a special friend that he tells in his own words at my request. I find his experience a powerful sermon.

"It was the third Saturday in January a few years ago. I was excited to attend a seminar that morning. It was an agriculture seminar at Brigham Young University, where I had been attending school. I had been home from my Honolulu Hawaii Mission six months and was going through all the adjustments of a returned missionary. The challenge of family, girls, school, and the fact that there were 25,000 other students who were bright and aggressive—some with plenty of money; others, like myself, who were pinching every nickel—didn't make things easier.

"I landed a job earlier that week running a hydraulic press in a machine shop. We made seals for hydraulic equipment. Following the seminar that morning, I went to work. Kimball, my roommate and former missionary companion who had gone to work earlier that morning, instructed me in how to make a new seal. After approximately twenty minutes, one of the smallest seals stuck on the face of the plate. I struggled to get it off with my left hand. As I turned back to give it my full attention and use my right hand, the machine closed on my left hand, causing a horrible noise as it crushed my hand just below the wrist. After what seemed an eternity, the huge press finally opened. My first thought when I looked at my hand was 'What a mess!' Then that inner voice which I had come to know, love, and appreciate whispered, 'Jerry, you won't have your hand.'

"Four hours of surgery followed. The first thing I remember hearing was the surgeon's voice in the recovery room.

"'Jerry,' he said, 'can you hear me?'

"'Yes,' I said.

"'We had to take your hand off.'

"The following four days were filled with tears, aches, friends, cards, letters, and family. Concerned people made it so much easier for me, especially Kimball. He let my parents and others close to me know and helped in every way he could. Never did I have to ask for one thing. It was already done. By his example and support, he gave me courage to face this new challenge.

"The days in the hospital were filled with painful, sleepless hours and nights. Those nights gave me an opportunity to think about the Savior and Joseph Smith as I had never done before. I reviewed the Prophet Joseph's life from everything I had learned. He faced physical, emotional, and spiritual trial upon trial. How I marveled at his well-won victories. At this difficult time I promised the Lord I would try to accept all of my challenges as the Prophet Joseph had accepted his.

"Of course, during the first night there were thoughts of 'Why me? Was it something in my past? What have I done to deserve this?' Then I thought, 'No more rodeo, football, or skiing,' and I wondered what type of woman would want a one-handed husband. I hadn't developed a good self-image or a great deal of self-esteem, so these thoughts magnified my concerns.

"Mom came to school and drove me home for the weekend. One thing she said that made me again appreciate her greatness was, 'Jerry, if I could only give you my left hand and make it work, I would.'

"Sunday was fast Sunday. As I stood favoring my bandaged, shortened arm, I thanked everyone for their thoughts, prayers, and cards. I realized as never before that good friends and faithful family members make challenges less difficult.

"After the testimony meeting, an admired friend gave me a special blessing. So many questions were answered during his blessing. He told me this accident was not punishment for anything I had done but, rather, an opportunity to help me become a better person and to amplify those particular traits which needed to be developed. He shared the thought that this challenge could make me more understanding of people, problems, and life. As I look back now, each point of his blessing and encouragement has helped in a very fulfilling way.

"One of my greatest fears was the constant thought of how people would accept me. Would they be afraid of me, question my ability, or write me off before I could prove myself? Would girls turn down dates because I was different? Would it make them feel uncomfortable to be seen with me?

"I had dated several girls since my mission but had dated Julie only a couple of times. When I awoke the day following the operation in the hospital, she was there with other friends. I asked everyone else to leave the room, and I then proceeded to give her what I thought was the perfect speech. I told her that they had to take my hand off. If she felt embarrassed or ashamed to be with me or be seen with me on future dates, she need not feel obligated to continue in any future courtship. At that moment I could see fire in her eyes. She let me know in no uncertain terms that she was not there out of pity or duty, but only because she cared for me. She indicated she would help me, but never feel sorry for

me. Six months later we were married in the Salt
Lake Temple.

"There were many job interviews, prejudices,
and rejections of employment; but with continued
encouragement, the Lord blessed us in innumerable
ways. When our first girl, Bracken, arrived, we were
left short of money to go to school. So after a major
decision, we went into business, which proved to be
another learning experience. After a couple of years
with many reverses, I was able to find a career in personnel management, which fulfilled not only my
goals, but answered my prayers.

"Today as I look back, I see the challenge of adversity as something upon which to build. Of course,
I cannot say the experience was pleasant; it was horrible. However, I hope I have used this adversity in a
positive way. When I see others in trouble, in pain,
when real adversity is knocking, I have an opportunity not only to feel something of what they feel, but
perhaps I can also help them because they can see
that I have challenges of my own."

Following a recent discussion on the subject of
adversity, a young man who was greatly concerned
about the burdens being carried by his wonderful
mother asked the question, "If God is omnipotent
and knows all, why does He put my mother through
the agony of continual sufferings when He already
knows what the outcome will be?" Our response was,
"Your mother's trials are not tests so the Lord can
measure her. They are tests and trials so that your
mother can measure herself. It is most important
that she know her strengths in adversity and grow
from the experiences."

When, with several companions, the Prophet

Joseph Smith was a prisoner in Liberty, Missouri, for a number of months, conditions were deplorable. Petitions and appeals directed to executive officers and the judiciary had failed to bring relief. In desperation Joseph pleaded for understanding and assistance from his Heavenly Father. The message finally came:

"My son, peace be unto thy soul; thine adversity and thine afflictions shall be but a small moment: And then, if thou endure it well, God shall exalt thee on high; thou shalt triumph over all thy foes." (D&C 121:7-8.)

It can be declared accurately and without hesitation that Joseph Smith's noble character and stature were shaped and achieved by constant victories over his afflictions. Jesus, too, developed unique balance mentally, physically, spiritually, and socially as He labored and served under all types of trying circumstances. "Though he were a Son, yet learned he obedience by the things which he suffered; and being made perfect, he became the author of eternal salvation unto all them that obey him." (Hebrews 5:8-9.)

Difficulties can be a valuable tool in our pursuit of perfection. Adversity need have no necessary connection with failure. Proper self-management and self-discipline in all of our trials can bring strength. If we are prepared, we can meet life's challenges victoriously. We become His disciples when we continue faithfully under all circumstances, including suffering and tragedy.

C. S. Lewis shared a meaningful observation when he said, "I have seen great beauty of spirit in some who were great sufferers. I have seen men, for the most part, grow better not worse with advancing years, and I have seen the last illness produce treasures of fortitude and meekness from most unpromising subjects."

I have another choice friend who has known very few days in his life that were not filled with pain, discomfort, or disease. He shakes his fists at the forces of darkness and trial. His taxing trials of all of the yesterdays have been properly met and have assisted in making him what he is today. Like Caleb of old, he, too, can be heard to say, "As yet I am . . . strong. . . . Now therefore give me this mountain." (Joshua 14:11-12.) More mountains, even those high in adversity, can better prepare us for tomorrow if we are but willing to climb.

Jesus Christ, the Master, shares his life of trials and victories with us for our motivation and direction. God strengthened His son. He, too, will support us, His children, if we will turn to Him for guidance.

What a blessing it is to know that we can be supported against all the fiery darts of the enemy if we are faithful. A worthy daily prayer is one asking for the power to be faithful under all circumstances.

Knowing that Satan and his hosts are relentless in their attempts to ridicule, embarrass, belittle, and cause all of us to yield and ultimately fall, what should be our attitude in today's society? An important step that goes beyond avoiding contention and strife is to live with dignity. There is something sacred about living with dignity. We need not quarrel or compete with those who promote and encourage controversy. We need not spend our time in retaliation. They who would deceive, destroy, or belittle reap their own rewards. Their works are neither praiseworthy nor of good report. How disarming it must be to the enemies to see the valiant moving forward with poise and dignity under all challenging circumstances. Scorn and ridicule are two of the greatest forms of adversity we are required to face in today's world. Doing the will of God on a daily basis leaves no time for contention or confrontation.

From Harry Emerson Fosdick we read, "The most extraordinary thing about the oyster is this. Irritations get into his shell. He does not like them. But when he cannot get rid of them, he uses the irritation to do the loveliest thing an oyster ever has a chance to do. If there are irritations in our lives today, there is only one prescription: make a pearl. It may have to be a pearl of patience, but anyhow, make a pearl. And it takes faith and love to do it."

Those who yield to adversity become weaker. To the valiant it is a stepping-stone to increased power. Members of The Church of Jesus Christ of Latter-day Saints and God-fearing people worldwide will not pray for freedom from trials. They will not surrender or panic. They will strive to put themselves in condition to meet and master troublesome trials.

Usually there are no easy answers to most of our problems. Each individual must think, plan, work, and pray to find the help he needs and the courage he must have to conquer his problem or carry his cross, whatever his lot may be. Winners set achievable goals day by day. Their plans consist of things that can be done, not what can't be done. They remember that God has not given us the spirit of fear, but the power of love and of a sound mind.

God seems to have sustaining love for those like Jerry who are coping courageously with adversity. In many cases it seems they have a special relationship with Him. "Behold, I have refined thee, . . . I have chosen thee in the furnace of affliction." (Isaiah 48:10.)

Each of us should thank God for the examples of those about us who battle and conquer daily challenges that are intense, real, and continuing. There are some persons who seem to have more than their share of trouble, as we measure with our human eyes, but with God's help they are made special. They will not break. They will not yield. Satan wants us to feel unequal to our worldly tasks. If we turn to God, He will take us by the hand and lead us through our darkest hours. To these truths I bear my testimony.

Look Up
to the
Temple

Temples
give us a chance
to extend our vision,
to look
to our tomorrows
as well as
our todays

In my personal journal on October 10, 1977, is recorded: "Today I had the opportunity of taking President Kimball, President Tanner, and President Romney to three prospective temple sites in Sandy, Riverton, and South Jordan [Utah]. After we walked up the hill to the west on the Holt property, the last we were to visit, I said to President Kimball as we stood alone—President Tanner and President Romney were together on another part of the property—'President Kimball, how do you feel about this location?' He said, 'I like it. I will discuss it with my counselors.' The last line in my journal entry continues, 'I am under the impression this is where a temple will be built.'"

On a fall evening in 1981, just prior to the dedication of the beautiful Jordan River Temple, Sister Ashton and I toured the temple with a special family, which included a mother, father, son, and three daughters, Hope, Lisa, and Anne. As the family made their way out the front entry, one of the girls said within my hearing, "We've got to walk down the road a ways so we can look up at the temple." I watched with keen interest as they looked up at that holy structure in its majestic splendor and unmatched setting. They seemed fascinated not only by the lighting and the beauty, but in anticipation of coming again for their own purposes.

Temples give us a chance to extend our vision. Temples should cause all of us to look up, not down, not back. The gospel of Jesus Christ should cause us to look up. The light of the truth and way should cause us to constantly look up.

Isaiah wrote, "Lift up your eyes on high." (Isaiah 40:26.) We read in Psalms, "I will lift up mine eyes unto the hills, from whence cometh my help." (Psalm 121:1.) In Third Nephi we read, "Lift up your head and be of good cheer; for behold, the time is at hand." (3 Nephi 1:13.) And finally, "Behold, I am the law, and the light. Look unto me, and endure to the end, and ye shall live; for unto him that endureth to the end will I give eternal life." (3 Nephi 15:9.)

One of the main reasons we build temples is so that people can look up to them. There is great good in store for those who make their ways worthily and properly motivated. To look up properly prepared mentally and spiritually is not only a challenge, but also a tremendous blessing. If we are properly motivated and challenged, oftentimes our preparations and looking forward to attending the temple can be as important as our entry. A well-planned journey is often as rewarding as the arrival to enter the doors. With this type of planning and attitude, when we come out of the temple, we are really on our way back. The memory of the covenants and spirit prepare us to come and go more effectively. We can look to tomorrow with more purpose and joyous anticipation.

Temples give us a chance to look to those whom we can serve.

Some time ago on a July Sunday morning, I accompanied my nine-year-old grandson to Temple Square in Salt Lake City to attend the Tabernacle Choir broadcast. As we came from the Church parking lot, he looked up at the temple. "What is that building, Jeff?" I asked. He gave me one of those looks that only a nine-year-old can give you when you have asked a five-year-old question. He said, "It's the temple." And so I wouldn't have to back off entirely, I said, "What are temples for?" He answered, "It's where I'm going to get married someday."

Thank God for caring parents who teach their children early in their lives to look forward to the temple!

Temples should cause us to look to our tomorrows. Temples should cause us to look to our todays. Temples should cause us to look to those whom we can serve. A chance to serve those about us, ourselves, and those who have gone ahead is a worthy destination.

In our preparations to go to the temple, we should never forget that we can help others on our way. What a joy it is to help friends, old and new, to look to the temple as an important step in their eternal lives. Not long ago we had an opportunity to accompany a family to the temple—a mother and father and three children—to witness the joy of those being sealed to them for time and eternity. Two years later two of their sons were serving in the mission field.

In the New Testament we read: "Now Peter and John went up together into the temple at the hour of prayer, being the ninth hour. And a certain man lame from his mother's womb was carried, whom they laid daily at the gate of the temple which is called Beautiful, to ask alms of them that entered into the temple; who seeing Peter and John about to go into the temple asked an alms.

"And Peter, fastening his eyes upon him with John, said, Look on us. And he gave heed unto them, expecting to receive something of them. Then Peter said, Silver and gold have I none; but such as I have give I thee: In the name of Jesus Christ of Nazareth rise up and walk. And he took him by the right hand, and lifted him up: and immediately his feet and ancle bones received strength. And he leaping up stood, and walked, and entered with them into the temple, walking, and leaping, and praising God.

"And all the people saw him walking and praising God: and they knew that it was he which sat for alms at the Beautiful gate of the temple: and they were filled with wonder and amazement at that which had happened unto him.

"And as the lame man which was healed held Peter and John, all the people ran together unto them in the porch that is called Solomon's, greatly wondering. And when Peter saw it, he answered unto the people, Ye men of Israel, why marvel ye at this? or why look ye so earnestly on us, as though by our own power or holiness we had made this man to walk?" (Acts 3:1-12.)

We too can take others with us to the temple. We can prepare them. We can lift them. We can accompany them—those who are in need, hungry, helpless, or cold, even those temporarily lost.

Temples give us a chance to look to our commitments. As we think of our lives, our attitudes, and our future service, let the word *commitment* take on new depth and significance. Commit means *to do*. Commitment in the temple isn't an agreement to hear, to see, to witness, or to renew. It is an agreement *to do*. It is a personal agreement to do the will of the Lord, to stand up and be counted in righteousness, and to walk firmly in His paths. Often the personal decisions and commitments made in the temple determine the course of our lives. Those attending temple sessions will spend their time appropriately if they not only serve those who have gone ahead of them, but also give their hearts and minds spiritual refreshment of communication, courage, and commitment. The opportunity to look, meditate, and learn is priceless.

These blessings and strengths are available to all of us each time we attend a session in the temple. We can all be grateful for the great leveling influence in temple ordinance attendance. As we attend temple sessions, we are reminded there is no high, there is no low, there is no rich, there is no poor, just God's children, brothers and sisters united in a common, selfless purpose. Thankfully God looks to us as temple attenders and nothing more or less than what we truly are.

Temples give us a chance to look to houses of prayer. "My house shall be called the house of prayer." (Matthew 21:13.) "This house may be a house of prayer, a house of fasting, a house of faith, a house of glory and of God, even thy house." (D&C 109:16.) "And verily I say unto you, let this house be built unto my name, that I may reveal mine ordinances therein unto my people." (D&C 124:40.)

Look to the temple as a place of rejoicing. The choice words of Charles Wesley in our hymn "Rejoice, the Lord Is King" express this well:

> *Rejoice, the Lord is King!*
> *Your Lord and King adore!*
> *Mortals give thanks and sing*
> *And triumph evermore.*
>
> *His kingdom cannot fail!*
> *He rules o'er earth and heaven.*
> *The keys of death and hell*
> *To Christ the Lord are given.*
>
> *Lift up your heart!*
> *Lift up your voice!*
> *Rejoice again; I say, rejoice!*
> *Lift up your heart!*
> *Lift up your voice!*
> *Rejoice again; I say, rejoice!*

May God help us to look up to the temple for light, beauty, and strength; to look to the temple to extend our vision, to serve others, to renew our commitments; to come to the temple and learn to really know how to pray; to come to the temple to rejoice and praise God.

Give with Wisdom That They May Receive with Dignity

Welfare services
in the Church
provide opportunities
for one person
to work with another
to the
mutual betterment
of both

During a session of Education Week sponsored by Brigham Young University, a wise teacher and stake Relief Society president, Sister Leisel McBride, flashed a large picture on a screen. It showed a bright-eyed boy with unkempt hair and folded arms, deep in thought. The caption read, "I know I'm somebody 'cause God don't make no junk."

With the grammar improved, that caption could well be the theme of welfare services in the Church.

Every human being in every walk of life needs help in building his self-respect and self-reliance. To be truly effective, welfare services must be concerned with the betterment of the total individual. A person's image of himself is nothing more nor less than what he has learned through his experiences and interactions with others. It is rewarding to note that someone has helped a typical boy develop his personal identity. Someone, perhaps a mother, a Primary teacher, or a neighbor, or even a song like "I Am a Child of God," had made this little boy realize he was someone. He knew he wasn't junk. He knew he wasn't impossible. He knew he was a human being loved by his Heavenly Father.

In Ecclesiastes 4:9-10 we read: "Two are better than one; because they have a good reward for their labour. For if they fall, the one will lift up his fellow:

but woe to him that is alone when he falleth; for he hath not another to help him up."

Proper application of welfare services principles is simply to provide opportunities for one person to work with another for the mutual betterment of both.

It was recently said of a teacher of the year, "He gives no answers to life's questions; rather, he directs each student to find his own answers. He doesn't make you feel dumb. He gives you confidence, encourages, doesn't push."

The welfare service arm of the Church was instituted to instill in all of us a feeling of individual worth by teaching and developing skills, self-sufficiency, and personal pride. It offers us the opportunity to serve and learn on a continuing basis. Through it we can learn the lessons of never giving up on ourselves or others, never being defeated by our situations.

The only time we fail in any activity is when we give up on each other. Patience, long-suffering, and true love can best be taught and learned as we become anxiously engaged in trying to lift all of God's children.

One day following a Sunday School class, a teacher asked me to shake hands with a special child. As I held my hand out and greeted the boy, I became aware that perhaps the only meaningful thing this child could do was carry the teacher's books to class. What did this empathic teacher have the boy doing? Carrying her books. Thank God for leaders who know how to teach self-reliance on a level commensurate with the capabilities of those they lead.

Robert Louis Stevenson used these words to remind us of this fact: "To be what we are, and to become what we are capable of becoming, is the only end of life." (*Familiar Studies of Men and Books,* 1882.) Our Savior said it this way, "As my Father hath sent me, even so I send you." (John 20:21.) Each one has something special to live for. Some can find their special niche by themselves, but many need additional help. All of us are a part of this inspired welfare activity as we assist each other in fulfilling our purposes here on earth.

Satan will do his best to deter us and let discouragement impede our progress. Through trying times we would do well to remember and repeat the famous words of Sir Winston Churchill, England's Lion of Courage, during some of his country's darkest days. With character and strength peculiar to himself, he said, "Never give in, never give in, *never, never, never, never.*" This mighty statesman in his own way was echoing the words of another mighty leader: "If ye continue in my word, then are ye my disciples indeed; and ye shall know the truth, and the truth shall make you free." (John 8:31-32.)

Paul Harvey, news analyst and author, said, "Someday I hope to enjoy enough of what the world calls success so that someone will ask me, 'What's the secret of it?' I shall say simply this: 'I get up when I fall down.'"

There are those who would have us believe that the present welfare services principles are outdated, overemphasized, and impossible under existing world conditions. To them we would declare it is easier for some skeptics to give up than to learn. It is no doubt easier to be a critic than a servant. In the uncertain days of the present and of the future, welfare services will remain a beacon for the world to see. Its very foundation continues to be built upon the rock of helping people to help themselves. Properly implemented, most human needs can be met through this important program of the Church.

Welfare services is God's way. We must have this belief and trust if we are to properly involve ourselves. Besides materials, commodities, money, supplies, labor, and skills, there must be faith—faith to help, faith to lead, and faith to obey in God's way. For guidance and strength, may we refer to the words of the Savior: "I, the Lord, stretched out the heavens, and built the earth, my very handiwork; and all things therein are mine. . . . But it must needs be done in mine own way; and behold this is the way that I, the Lord, have decreed to provide for my saints, that the poor shall be exalted, in that the rich are made low." (D&C 104:14, 16.)

Self-reliance is developed through a proper balance of agency and accountability. As we live, teach, and share, we develop self-reliance in ourselves and others.

For welfare services to be viable and successful, every member of the Church must be appropriately involved. The Lord's way always involves the individual, the family, and the Church working together. A close tie between welfare services and the home is a necessity. Human understanding, wise preparation, and guidance through prayer are essential ingredients. For order and effectiveness, all action should be taken through proper channels. It is not enough to make elaborate plans, set up programs, and give serious thought to preparation. Most of us can do that, but many have a hard time really practicing the principles we believe. Some of us have a tendency to shun the fight.

The strongest helping hand is most often the one closest to ourselves—our very own hands. Do you consider your own options for self-help as problems arise? Or do you toss your arms in the air and say "Oh, no!" or "Why me?" Do you quietly sit down, review the facts, and list all the possible courses of action? Do you identify causes and determine remedies? Quiet contemplation can solve problems more quickly than frantic force.

President Marion G. Romney has said so often, "No self-respecting Church member will voluntarily shift the responsibility for his own maintenance to another. Furthermore, a man not only has the responsibility to care for himself; he also has the responsibility to care for his family." (*Ensign*, May 1981, p. 88.) Paul, speaking to this point, said, "But if any provide not for his own, and specially for those of his own house, he hath denied the faith, and is worse than an infidel." (1 Timothy 5:8.)

The home, which is the heart of welfare services, and its members should be involved so that self-respect may be maintained. We must constantly bear in mind that if the total well-being of the individual is to be realized, all members in the family must participate.

Family members usually understand each other best. By working as a team, they may see problems from different points of view. When family councils can be held without destructive arguments, new and better solutions to challenging situations may become evident. Pooling of efforts and resources gives family members a chance to reap the rewards of con-

fidence and security as they help one another solve
problems and make progress toward self-reliance
and accountability.

Of course, there are times when some of us
must turn to Church resources for help. What a
comfort it is to know such resources are available
when the needs cannot be met by the individual or
his family. Here, too, action is to be taken through
proper channels, which are well defined. Emotion
or panic do not determine the path to follow. All
things are to be done in the Lord's own way as
specified by our modern-day prophets.

One of the most rewarding projects for the individual and the family is to avoid debt whenever possible. Debt in itself is neither good nor bad; it is a
financial tool with the potential of being either. Debt
in business may be used to increase productivity or
aid in expansion. However, individuals in debt are
often average people who are temporarily out of
financial control. The victims of poor monetary
habits, they often have no idea of the importance of
proper money management. They misuse credit,
especially credit cards, and don't live within budgets
or wise operational guidelines. For many of us, credit is like a magic carpet on which we can fly to places
we couldn't ordinarily get to. We ride free at first,
forgetting that a little later we will have to pay for the
magic carpet. Bondage-producing interest rates
added to the original amount will turn out to be stag-
gering.

Debt can cause serious family conflict. Often
couples who have trouble stretching their paychecks
find their marriage stretched to the breaking point.
Debt can be destructive, causing financial bondage,

bankruptcy, and the loss of self-respect. A family that manages money wisely and budgets well, including tithing and fast offerings, is helping itself and others in the Lord's own way. Just debts should be paid. I believe the Lord wants us to be successful in our honorable occupational pursuits and to use wisely our means for the benefit of the individual, family, church, and community.

The practice of thrift is not outdated. We must discipline ourselves to live within our incomes even if it means going without or making do. The wise person can distinguish between basic needs and extravagant wants. Some find budgeting extremely painful, but I promise you, it is never fatal.

Jesus said, "Feed my sheep." (John 21:16.) We can't feed them if we don't know where they are. We can't feed them if we give them reason to resist us. We can't feed them if we don't have the food. We can't feed them if we don't have charity. We can't feed them if we aren't willing to work and share.

Wherever these lost sheep may be, a necessary ingredient for helping is empathy, the ability to understand someone else's feelings and to feel what he feels. Meaningful help can never be given without empathy for the recipient. This requires gaining the confidence of the person; listening with eyes, ears, and heart; trying to comprehend how this person feels; and then letting him know by our personal performance that we really understand. One who really understands and is empathic doesn't solve another's problems, doesn't argue, doesn't top his story, doesn't make accusations, doesn't take away free agency. He merely helps the person build his self-reliance and self-image so he can try to find his own solutions.

Those who need help come in all age brackets. Some of His sheep are young, lonely, and lost. Some are weary, afflicted, and worn with age. Some are in our own families, in our own neighborhoods, or in the far corners of the world where we can help with fast offerings. Some are starving for food; some are starving for love and concern.

If we give His sheep reasons to resist us, the feeding process becomes difficult, if not impossible. No one can teach or help with sarcasm or ridicule. Dictatorship or "I'm right and you are wrong" will negate all efforts to feed a wandering sheep. A wall of resistance will be built, and no one will benefit.

We must never encourage someone to do something that causes him to lose his pride, or he will turn away and we will have lost the opportunity to help. May we also bear in mind that we never give one of God's children a lift when we give him a free ride. Every person in the Church should possess a self-sustaining spirit of independence that insists he work for what he receives. The best foods with which to feed His sheep are charity and dignity.

By our actions we show our love. Expressions of affection are empty if actions don't match. All His sheep need the touch of a shepherd who cares, who leads His flock along upward paths where they can see the value of walking in obedience to God's laws and feel the dignity of reaching lofty goals.

Charity should start in our own homes. Too many of us extend charity to others when it is often most needed within the family circle.

An old Serbian proverb says, "Kindness is the only service that power cannot command and money cannot buy." The best way to show our love in caring and feeding is to take time to prove it with kindness hour by hour and day by day. True love is as eternal as life itself.

While President Spencer W. Kimball was recovering from a recent illness, I heard many members of the Church express their love and gratitude for him. Many were looking for ways to show sincere gratitude to him for his service and selfless love. From a priceless, intimate association with President Kimball, I think I can give some guidelines: learn to love, unconditionally, all of God's children, regardless of race, creed, or color, and try to serve as President Kimball serves. This principle is the foundation of service. Each of us could do well to remember this scripture: "He that is ordained of God and sent forth, the same is appointed to be the greatest, notwithstanding he is the least and the servant of all." (D&C 50:26.)

The Lord cares enough about us to give us direction for serving and the opportunity for developing self-reliance. His principles are consistent and never changing. Practices may be altered as situations warrant, but the Lord's principles are ever stable. The success of service in the Church depends on obedience to the basic gospel laws upon which it is built. There is room for innovation and use of free agency when we look for wise ways to serve as long as we stay within the framework of the gospel.

May God help us to give of ourselves with wisdom that they may receive with dignity. Truly, "God makes no junk." We are his children. He loves us and wants us to love ourselves, our families, and our neighbors in a meaningful way. The welfare services program is an inspired way of life. It is the implementation of eternal principles for the welfare and benefit of all mankind.

Be Not
Weary in
Well-doing

May we learn
from children:
They may become tired,
they may become
mischievous,
but I've never seen
a child who wearied
in well-doing

Afew years ago during an assignment to Sao Paulo, Brazil, I had the opportunity of visiting in the home of a seminary leader. While Brother and Sister David Christensen were in the kitchen making final preparations for the evening meal, I was in the living room alone with seven-year-old Julie. I asked her, "Julie, whom do you love more than anyone else?"

She said, "My mommy."

"Why?"

"She loves me."

"Who else do you love?"

"My daddy."

"Why?"

"He loves me a whole bunch too."

A few minutes later as we sat in the living room together, she said, "Brother Ashton, my mommy and my daddy and I think that if you would give my little brother Carey a blessing he could get better. He's two years old. He can't see very well. He isn't growing very much. He can't walk around the house without falling. He's almost blind."

Later as her father and I prepared to give Carey a blessing, I noticed Julie, arms folded, seated quietly and reverently in her little chair. When our prayer was over, Julie said, "He's going to get better, isn't he, Brother Ashton?"

Some two years later the Christensens came to

my office—mother, father, Julie, and Carey. Carey, now four, was walking, jumping, and running. He was so wiggly that his parents were embarrassed. I thought of the experience of the Savior:

"At the same time came the disciples unto Jesus, saying, Who is the greatest in the kingdom of heaven? And Jesus called a little child unto him, and set him in the midst of them, and said, Verily I say unto you, Except ye be converted, and become as little children, ye shall not enter into the kingdom of heaven. Whosoever therefore shall humble himself as this little child, the same is greatest in the kingdom of heaven. And whoso shall receive one such little child in my name receiveth me." (Matthew 18:1-5.)

I know the power of the priesthood, particularly in this administration as given to this ailing young boy. I also bear witness of the power of a seven-year-old Primary girl. Truly, out of small things—children—proceedeth that which is great.

We are living in days when it is easy to be discontented, tired, fatigued, bored, and vexed in and with life. Discouragement and weariness set in when we allow ourselves a dangerous luxury of self-pity. Such thoughts as these come to us when we allow ourselves to become discouraged and weary: "No one appreciates you." "Even your own children won't listen to you." "You don't have to get involved with someone else." "You're really not accomplishing anything." "Why should I serve when others who have so much more to offer are not serving?" And even a whispering such as, "Why should you teach when your own home isn't in order?"

The attitude with which we approach our calls in the Church controls the outcome. God has not

called us and selected us totally for what we are as
potential leaders, but because of what we may become in the days ahead.

Have you ever thought that some reverses and
some heartaches in your own family can make you
more understanding and successful as a teacher and
a leader? The only time we fail in the home is when
we give up on family members, and the only time we
fail in our church callings is when we give up on class
members, associates, and ourselves—when we become weary in well-doing.

One of the last meaningful contacts I had with
President Harold B. Lee, a man whom I revere and
love with all my heart, was when he met with me and
handed me a little note, which said, "Dear Marv,
Here is another troubled mother and Primary
leader. Perhaps you can give her some counsel as to
how she might cope with her problem or seek aid
from those who are near her who are in a position to
help. Sincerely yours, Harold B. Lee." This is the letter he gave me:

Dear President Lee:
    I've been meaning to write to you for some time, but hesi-
tated to burden you further with problems of this day. However, it seems to be getting the best of me. The problem, of
course, is with our children.
    To begin with, I am a stake Primary president. My hus-
band is in my opinion one of the best Scoutmasters in the
Church. But we seem to have failed with our own children. We
have three boys. Our oldest is twenty-two years old. Several
months ago he returned from the service. Since he's come
home he's lost his girl, lost his job, and seems unfeeling, uncar-
ing, unable to assume any responsibility. I have become frustrated in working with him trying to encourage him. My husband says to leave him alone and let him find himself and to
stop worrying, though I know he does, too. Many times I've

told myself to stop, too, but it does no good. We have an eighteen-year-old who had a brilliant future but now seems to be drifting away from us and the Church.

Our youngest is twelve. He is active in Scouting and seems to love the priesthood. But the others did too at his age. I get the greatest feeling of depression when I think of his future and wonder what we as parents are doing wrong in our teaching. My parents and my husband's parents were never active; our life was going to be different—we *took* our children with us. But it has apparently done no good.

How do I find peace of mind? How can we live with this? What can we do for them? Should I resign from the Primary? How do we get the 'divine inner spark' that helps us face trouble and grief? I have become weary, tired—yes, discouraged. But there seems to be no way to live with it when you know you failed. Sincerely. . . .

This is what I wrote her:

Dear Sister,

President Lee has asked me to respond to your recent letter. We share your concern for your sons, but it would be unwise for me to attempt to speculate as to why they are having problems.

However, one thing does concern me about your letter. You speak of your feelings of failure and discouragement. This is Satan's greatest weapon. Peace only comes through the Spirit of Christ and through steadfastness in serving the Lord. May I suggest that your sorrow could help make you an even more effective Primary worker and your husband, who is already a good Scoutmaster, better and more sensitive to the special needs of boys. The Savior is totally understanding and merciful. You can expect him to treat you with infinite mercy, and you in turn can treat your prodigal sons the same way.

Finally, may we suggest that you rely upon your good husband as well as your bishop for counsel, and realize we must not give up on our family members or ourselves. Ever bear in mind that the only time we fail in our homes and in the Church is when we give up on each other.

Our prayers are in your behalf. Sincerely, Marvin J. Ashton.

Do not weary in well-doing. We can frustrate Satan if we weary not.

More than thirty years ago my father wrote of an experience one of his sons was having with his Primary teacher. I think this report carries a powerful lesson and fits well into our theme of today. This report is entitled "Mother, That's the Best Teacher in the World."

One night he came home from Primary. (Thank goodness for the boy's honesty.) He told us this story:—I guess he talked too much in Primary. The teacher stood it as long as she could and then had to do something about it. As I got this story, the teacher called his attention to the fact that he was making too much noise and asked him if he hadn't better step out of the class and think things over. He did. Of course as his parent I wanted him to do his part to rectify the same. Calling the lad by name I said, "Don't you think we had better go up to the teacher's home tonight and talk things over?" The boy agreed with me and that was our plan for the evening.

Well, I went on with my work in the garden, and pretty soon the sun started to go back over the horizon, and the shades of night began to fall. It was then that I had the shock of my life. I guess the lad thought I had forgotten the call we were to make on his Primary teacher that night. I had a gentle pull at my coattail reminding me that we were going to make the call.

Now let me pause right here for a moment. When I was a lad and if I had had this experience with my father when I was in Primary, I would have done anything but pray that my father would forget about the visit we were going to make to the teacher with whom we had had some trouble.

Well, to make the story short, we went up that night, and the boy did all the talking, and the teacher gave him another chance. Yes, but in a few days the same thing happened again. Too much talking and the boy was invited again to leave the room to get hold of himself. I was sure the right thing to do again was to visit his teacher. Calling the boy by name I said, "Now you had better go up and see her, and you ask her if she will give you one more chance." He did, and she did. A couple of weeks after, this fellow came home to his mother with this explanation: He said, "Mother, that's the best Primary teacher in the world." His mother, of course, realizing the trouble he had had with the Primary teacher, wondered why such an observation should come from him in the emphatic terms expressed. "Why?" said she. If you are as well acquainted with boys as some of us are, you will know that a lad, with respect to a horse, as far as water and feed are concerned, the horse should live on air. I guess this boy of ours was no exception to the rule. He had staked his horse out in the field, and of course between ball games and marbles he had forgotten that particular day that the animal existed. He said, "You know, Mother, that teacher carried two buckets of water to my horse up in the field." It seemed that the boy had staked the horse out near the home of this particular Primary teacher about whom we are speaking.

May I stop long enough right here to take my hat off, if you please, to that Primary teacher. Notwithstanding the trouble she had with that boy, she followed her real virtues when she went out of her way, on a busy summer day, to carry a bucket of water to a little Cayuse pony, and especially to the pony belonging to the boy who had caused her so much concern in the discipline of her Primary class.

I repeat, "Mother, that's the best teacher in the world." (Marvin O. Ashton, *To Whom It May Concern* [Bookcraft, 1946], pp. 187-89.)

We are leading and laying the foundation of a great work when we lead with patience and weary not.

I've spent considerable time the past few years working with a special friend of mine whom I met at the Utah State Prison. It's a continuing friendship, a continuing challenge. It's a great opportunity for me to weary not based on some of his conduct. But every time things get a little tough and a little tense and he becomes a little wayward, he looks at me and says, "Don't give up on me, friend," telling me in his own words not to weary.

"I have no greater joy than to hear that my children walk in truth." (3 John 1:4.) God has no greater joy than to see Church leaders and teachers joining hands with parents in walking with their children in truth. Let us resolve to be not weary in well-doing. The strong foundation of the great work we're laying will not only be for others, but as we build the foundation for others, our own foundation will be strengthened.

God grant us the courage and the strength to be not weary in well-doing. I pray that God will help us to frustrate the evil one by never yielding to the temptation of being weary. May we learn from children: They may become tired, they may become mischievous, but I've never seen a child who wearied in well-doing. May we learn from them, may we learn from each other, and may we learn from our Heavenly Father as we carry forward in our callings as parents and as leaders.

The Prophet
and
the Prison

What we can learn
from the example
of a modern prophet's
visit to a
state penitentiary

When our prophet Spencer W. Kimball and I walked through the admittance door of the Utah State Prison some time ago, the sound of sliding electronically controlled cell doors could be heard clanging in the background. The grating sounds of the steel bars against the concrete floors and walls let me know where I was again. The total situation was familiar to me. I had been in prison many times before—as a visitor. It was President Kimball's first visit. Once past the heavily guarded door, we were escorted to Warden Lawrence Morris's office near the front of the medium security area. Even after we were safely seated in his office, I had some real anxieties. I hoped conditions would be completely under control with no disturbances possible. There must not be any interference or interruption during the visit of the prophet. I was responsible for this trip, and as we sat there together, this situation weighed heavily upon me. Past experience had taught me that the behavior of some inmates is unpredictable. Fortunately the able warden had prepared well, and conditions in and around his office were calm and quiet. To my great relief, it appeared the grapevine means of communication inside the prison had not learned of the president's coming.

What had attracted President Kimball to the prison? Why was he there? What was his special interest? What was on his mind? Was there a certain inmate he wanted to see? Why should he expose himself to this dangerous environment when he had mountains of responsibilities needing attention in his own office?

With the prison visit over, and after time to reflect and ponder the situation, I now know President Kimball went there for many reasons and people. Being at his side and seeing him share himself with these special people will always be one of the choice experiences of my life. I learned much. I was with a prophet in an unstable environment. My senior companion, if you please, taught me well. As we traveled together to the prison, visited there, and returned in the car, the warmth and wisdom of this mighty man renewed in me a thrilling appreciation for his greatness.

Let me share with you some of the leadership traits I witnessed during this tour with President Kimball. As we review and think together, I hope we can apply these same traits in our lives. We can accomplish more and become stronger individually by following his example.

After a short visit in his office, the warden invited two inmates to come in and meet President Kimball. As they hesitatingly came in, President Kimball stood up, shook their hands, and gave them a warm welcome. I watched with keen interest. What would he say following the greeting? Perhaps others would have been inclined to say under these circumstances, "How long is your prison sentence? What was your crime? How long have you been here? Your family can't be very proud of you. You ought to be ashamed wasting your life in jail. Why don't you shape up?" President Kimball, however, said, "What are your special jobs out here? Where is your home? Tell me about your family. Are you working on the construction of the new chapel?" These were some of his questions, all of them free from criticism and embarrassment.

President Kimball set the example for me and for all of us as he conducted a "personal interview," if you please, with skill and sincerity. In a very few minutes, with few but appropriate words, he let two prisoners know he was with them because he cares.

When this short visit was over, we were to make our way to the new prison chapel, still under construction. Outside the temperature was near 40 degrees Fahrenheit. "Would you like to ride or walk the two-block distance?" President Kimball was asked. He responded with, "I would like to walk." Since he was without a topcoat, his personal secretary, D. Arthur Haycock, started to take his off to share with the president. President Kimball said, "No, thank you. You keep it on. If I walk, I won't need it." Just a routine gesture, perhaps, some could say, but to me it was evidence of President Kimball's courteous way of life.

As President Kimball walked to the new chapel site with wardens, prisoners, and a few others of us, I was close enough at hand to hear his constant questions and concerns. He listened intently as answers were given and situations of interest pointed out. I was impressed again with his concern for people, their confinement, and their treatment. At the chapel construction site he took time to shake hands with workers, some of whom were prisoners, and other visitors who were now aware of his presence.

He seemed to take time for everyone. People never seemed to be a bother. A number of workers jumped down from scaffolds to shake his hand. In some cases I saw his arm go out to them before they could clean dirt and mortar from their hands. They and leaders from other churches heard him say, "This interdenominational worship facility will help prisoners find their way back." He also added, "The Church and our people are happy to be participants in any and all community projects that are worthy." Once again I was impressed with his wholesome relationship with all people.

The highlight of the chapel inspection tour and the prison visit in general, it seemed to me, came when two inmates were invited to stand at the side of the prophet for picture taking in the minimum security reception area. As the president welcomed them and later put his arms around them, he said, "It is an honor for me to have my picture taken with you." The two prisoners were obviously touched by his comment. Others of us again saw the greatness and stature of one whom we love so much. Respect and human dignity were witnessed. Again he taught well that all people are entitled to be treated as human beings wherever they are found and without regard as to where they have been. President Kimball, it was obvious, is a foe of sin but a friend of the sinner. A verse of scripture found in the Doctrine and Covenants came forcefully to my mind: "He that is ordained of God and sent forth, the same is appointed to be the greatest, notwithstanding he is the least and the servant of all." (D&C 50:26.)

As we were finishing our visit, one inmate rushed up to me and said, "I didn't get a chance to shake President Kimball's hand. Would you please tell him I love him." Another prisoner commented "I'm not a Mormon, but he's got to be a special guy." Someday I hope he finds out what a special guy he really is.

Before we drove away from the prison compound, President Kimball viewed the maximum security area. When he looked at the extra fences, towers, guards, and isolated location, he commented on how unfortunate it is when men can't be given the responsibilities of freedom and the joys of work. "All men are basically good. Some just lose their way and need to be led back into proper paths and habits," he said.

President Kimball asked the warden how the Church's family home evening program was going at the prison. (He had been instrumental in its implementation there many years ago.) When told it was most successful, he was very pleased. He was informed that each week dozens of families continue to go to the prison on Monday evenings to provide family units for those qualified to be involved. These good people serve as families for inmates who don't have families. Their relationship, which often goes on after prisoners are released, provides an excellent anchor in rehabilitation. President Kimball has long been a believer that every person is entitled to family relationships, and when told some inmates have their first real family experiences through this program, he was delighted.

During the tour of the new chapel and the walk between the buildings, a number of men, young and old, were always nearby to assist and respond to President Kimball's questions. After hearing him refer to me a number of times as "Marv" as we walked together, one of the younger set was impressed to say, "Isn't it kind of neat to have President Kimball call you 'Marv'?" I responded with "Yes, it is, and it is especially neat to know that President Spencer W. Kimball is a prophet of God." I had again seen him in action.

In the car returning to Salt Lake City President Kimball thanked us time and again for taking him to the prison. He felt good about the response of those with whom he associated. "I hope you will make it possible for me to go back again," he suggested. "Those people need our love and constant encouragement."

What can we learn from President Kimball's trip to the prison? Much, I hope. Could I just quickly mention ten major points I observed. I think they can help us all be and do better if we will but follow his example.

1. He demonstrated how to interview "inactives," if you please, with friendly and sincere comments. His questions were free from embarrassment, ridicule, and criticism. How do you approach with words those whom you haven't seen for a while and want to reactivate?

2. He made others feel comfortable in his presence. He never talked down to anyone. He was always "one with" and not "one apart." Do we know how to make our associates comfortable during our visits, or are they allowed to feel we are just trying to improve our percentages?

3. He listened intently to the comments of his associates. Those about him knew they had his attention and interest. I thought of the scripture found in

Luke: "After three days they found him in the temple, sitting in the midst of the doctors, both hearing them, and asking them questions. And all that heard him were astonished at his understanding and answers." (Luke 2:46-47.) In this case perhaps we are within our rights to restructure this quotation a little and say, "After a few minutes they found him in the prison, sitting in the midst of the prisoners, both hearing them and asking them questions. And all that heard him were astonished at his capacity to ask and listen."

4. He was courteous. He knows well the fifth Boy Scout law and has undoubtedly been practicing it for more than seventy-five years.

5. He treated every person he met as a friend. He seemed to classify all whom he met into one category—basically good. Do you have the skill and capacity to be friendly to others when in your limited vision they may not seem to deserve it?

6. He expressed appreciation to everyone. No favor or assistance is ever taken for granted. "And in nothing doth man offend God, or against none is his wrath kindled, save those who confess not his hand in all things." (D&C 59:21.) Some who escape our love and association are starving for a word of encouragement and appreciation.

7. He exhibited a dignity, a poise, that was impressive. Governor Scott M. Matheson of the State of Utah was on hand during President Kimball's tour. As I walked, talked, and visited with both, I was greatly impressed with the fact that the governor received the same treatment from President Kimball as did the inmates. Do you have the capacity to love the inactive church member as much as you do the hundred percenter?

8. He despises sin but loves the sinner. When I saw his arms go around the shoulders of prisoners, I was touched. Are we beneath or above this type of behavior?

9. He is available to all of God's children. He made prisoners feel they were doing him a favor to let him have his picture taken with them. As I watched him in his personal associations, never once did I see him avoid a situation or an individual. When they wanted to shake his hand or have a picture, there was never "I'm tired" or "not now."

10. He took long and meaningful strides in the direction of all who were inclined to hesitate. He seems determined to bring back those on the edges. Do we have the same kind of continuing approach with those who are temporarily sidelined?

I am glad the time and conditions were right for President Kimball to visit his friends in prison and that I could be with him. One of the prisoners who stood at his side for the picture is serving time for theft and burglary; the other is there for manslaughter. One was a member, one a nonmember. His greeting to them, "It is an honor for me to have my picture taken with you," rings in my ears. "I was in prison, and ye came unto me." (Matthew 25:36.) Once again we have the heartwarming example of seeing how wide our president can spread his arms with love. He makes room for all of us. He will not give up on anyone.

It is my hope and prayer that we will all have the courage in our lives, homes, and quorums to lift, lead, and love as I saw demonstrated by a prophet in prison.

N. Eldon Tanner:
An Example
to Follow

President Tanner
is a Christian gentleman;
a courteous,
kind, and capable servant
of God;
a special witness
of the Savior
Jesus Christ

P

resident N. Eldon Tanner will go down in history as one of the greatest counselors ever to serve in the First Presidency of the Church. He has served with four presidents: David O. McKay, Joseph Fielding Smith, Harold B. Lee, and Spencer W. Kimball, and his performance has always been solid and significant. May I share some of his traits and strengths, hoping we can apply these principles in our daily lives for our total self-improvement.

Humility. As the First Presidency, the Council of the Twelve, and other General Authorities have met in the upper room of the temple on a once-a-month basis, President Kimball has never failed to call upon President Tanner to bear his testimony at the conclusion of these meetings. How often I have heard him say, "What am I doing here? I have so little to offer; I feel like I'm the least among you." In a spirit of true humility he asks, "What do I have to offer?" and he'll follow it by saying, "Nevertheless I pray every night and morning for God to help me to do my part. All I want in God's kingdom is to do what he wants me to do." In modestly accepting compliments, I have heard him say, "Now why would anyone want to say that about me?"

President Tanner follows closely the counsel in the Doctrine and Covenants: "Be thou humble; and the Lord thy God shall lead thee by the hand, and give thee answer to thy prayers." (D&C 112:10.) We would serve ourselves and others well if we could humbly say, "I don't know why I've been called, but I'm going to do the best I can." We should not let ourselves be concerned about our limitations or lack of talent; rather, we should resolve positively, with vigor and determination, to say, "I may not be much, I may not have much going for me, but in His strength, I can do all things." As I think of President Tanner, I see that humility is not a weakness—it is a strength. I have often heard him say, "God cannot answer our prayers unless we are humble."

Integrity. President Tanner is known by his associates in and out of the Church as Mr. Integrity, a man of character and quality, an advocate of self-discipline. Frequently in conference addresses he has admonished, "Be honest. Don't be a hypocrite. Be what you should be." He is a man of few words and much performance. I have never heard him make a cheap or shabby remark. I have never seen him when he was not a gentleman, when he was not the personification of integrity.

My first contact with President Tanner was in Canada in the 1950s, when he was president of the Calgary Stake. We had called a thirty-minute meeting for seven o'clock one evening to meet with stake leaders in the area. I remember well that night when seven o'clock arrived—and two of us were there. I was there as was a man I had never met before—N. Eldon Tanner. I will never forget the lesson I learned as I looked at my watch and then said to this man, "President Tanner, what do you suggest we do?" He replied, "You're here; I'm here; it's seven o'clock. Let's start."

Friendliness. President Tanner is a friend in the fullest sense of the word. He is a lifter, a builder, a leader. He is comfortable in any type of setting. I have never seen him when he did not fit in and when he did not make other people, no matter what the circumstances, feel welcome and happy to be in his company. He is willing to take people from where they are and help them forward from that point.

Caring. President Tanner's secretary, LaRue Sneff, once remarked that on occasion President Tanner has said to her, "In my office in the Church Office Building, I like to maintain such an atmosphere that those who come to call will go out feeling better than they did when they came in." We should all resolve to lift our associates under all circumstances. We all need to resist the temptation or the practice of cutting people down, even if we think they deserve it.

I will not soon forget an experience that took place shortly before Christmas one year. President Tanner called and said, "I have a letter here this morning from one of the inmates at the Utah State Prison. He wants to talk to me about something. Do you think you could arrange with the warden for me to talk with him on the phone? I don't think I'm going to have time to go and see him. Do you think you could arrange that?"

I replied, "President Tanner, I think I can. I have a few connections in the Utah State Prison." I called Warden Smith and arranged for this man to come out of maximum security and have the use of a telephone to talk to a President Tanner who had time for him. I don't know what they talked about—

I just made the appointment. But that is the kind of man N. Eldon Tanner is—a friend who truly cares regardless of where we are or what we have done.

Vision and vigor. A tireless, dedicated leader, President Tanner is about his Father's business early and late. I have never met a man with greater judgment or more superior wisdom.

In an honor banquet in Salt Lake City recognizing the lives and achievements of J. Willard Marriott and his wife, Alice, President Tanner said, "It is not because of the money the Marriotts have made or the great number of hotels they have built that we respect and admire them; it is because of the kind of lives they live. They have adopted the code 'Seek ye first the kingdom of God and his righteousness, and all these things shall be added unto you' and have lived it continually. The Church has benefitted greatly by them and their aid in the building of temples, chapels, buildings, and other things, and assisting worldwide in the great missionary effort."

The same might be said of N. Eldon Tanner. He believes in doing that which is right rather than that which is expedient. May we pursue proper priorities with vision and vigor as he does, and recall his comment when there are mighty decisions and responsibilities to perform: "All we have to do is what is right."

Selfless in service. In responding to the tribute paid him by President Tanner and others, Brother Marriott said, "President Tanner, you are a prime example of what a true Latter-day Saint can do for his church. When you came to Salt Lake City from Canada as a General Authority, you built a new home; before the paint was dry, you were called to serve a mission in Europe. Your service to the Church has always been outstanding."

President Tanner has always taken the time to serve in the community, the home, and the Church, whether it has been convenient or not. He was elected to the Alberta, Canada, provincial government and was named Speaker of the House. He then served in the provincial cabinet as head of the Department of Lands and Mines, one of the most important positions in Canadian government. In church and community, his skill and wisdom continue to benefit millions. He is truly a man among men.

Loyalty and devotion. President Tanner is a great husband, a wonderful father, and a worthy son. His loyal and supportive wife is his sweetheart and companion. All one has to do is be around President and Sister Tanner to see that they enjoy being with each other. She is his greatest advocate. One of his daughters has said, "All through Daddy's life he has found time for us and has always made us feel important." President Tanner has often given thanks for a father and mother who taught him to work and to have lofty goals. "My father taught me the virtue of dependability," he has said.

The words of a favorite Mormon hymn express well the philosophy of N. Eldon Tanner:

> *Have I done any good in the world today?*
> *Have I helped anyone in need?*
> *Have I cheered up the sad, and made someone feel*
> * glad?*
> *If not I have failed indeed.*

Has anyone's burden been lighter today,
Because I was willing to share?
Have the sick and the weary been helped on their way?
When they needed my help was I there?

There are chances for work all around just now,
Opportunities right in our way;
Do not let them pass by, saying, "Sometime I'll try,"
But go and do something today.
'Tis noble of man to work and to give,
Love's labor has merit alone;
Only he who does something is worthy to live,
The world has no use for the drone.

Then wake up, and do something more
Than dream of your mansion above;
Doing good is a pleasure, a joy beyond measure,
A blessing of duty and love.

— *Hymns,* no. 58

President Tanner is a Christian gentleman; a courteous, kind, and capable servant of God; a special witness of the Savior Jesus Christ; a man who rightly sits on the right-hand side of the prophet, Spencer W. Kimball; a man whose declaration "I know President Spencer W. Kimball is a prophet of God" carries profound significance, for who among earthly men knows the prophet better?

I thank my Heavenly Father for the life and example of President N. Eldon Tanner. I pray that all of us will try to incorporate in our lives the wonderful traits he exemplifies for us in his life. I love him with all my heart; I sustain and support him.

Index